GW01606081

RAYMOND RADIGUET

BY THE SAME AUTHOR

Cocteau's World: An Anthology of Writings by Jean Cocteau
Colette: The Difficulty of Loving
Jean Cocteau

MARGARET CROSLAND

RAYMOND RADIGUET

A Biographical Study
with Selections from His Work

PETER OWEN · LONDON

ISBN 0 7206 0413 3

This book has been published
with financial assistance from
the Arts Council of Great Britain.

PETER OWEN LIMITED
20 Holland Park Avenue London W11 3QU

First British Commonwealth edition 1976

Printed in Great Britain by
Daedalus Press Stoke Ferry King's Lynn Norfolk

Contents

Illustrations *(between pages 112 and 113)*

Acknowledgments

Many people have helped in the preparation of this book and I would like to thank especially Monsieur René Radiguet for the information and material he has so courteously supplied to me.

I am especially indebted to the books by David Noakes, Nadia Odouard and Francis Steegmuller mentioned in the Bibliography, to the editors of *Les Cahiers Jean Cocteau,* and to François Chapon, Keeper of the Bibliothèque Jacques Doucet.

I should also like to thank Peter Owen for his interest in Raymond Radiguet and Dan Franklin for his constructive editorial help.

M.C.

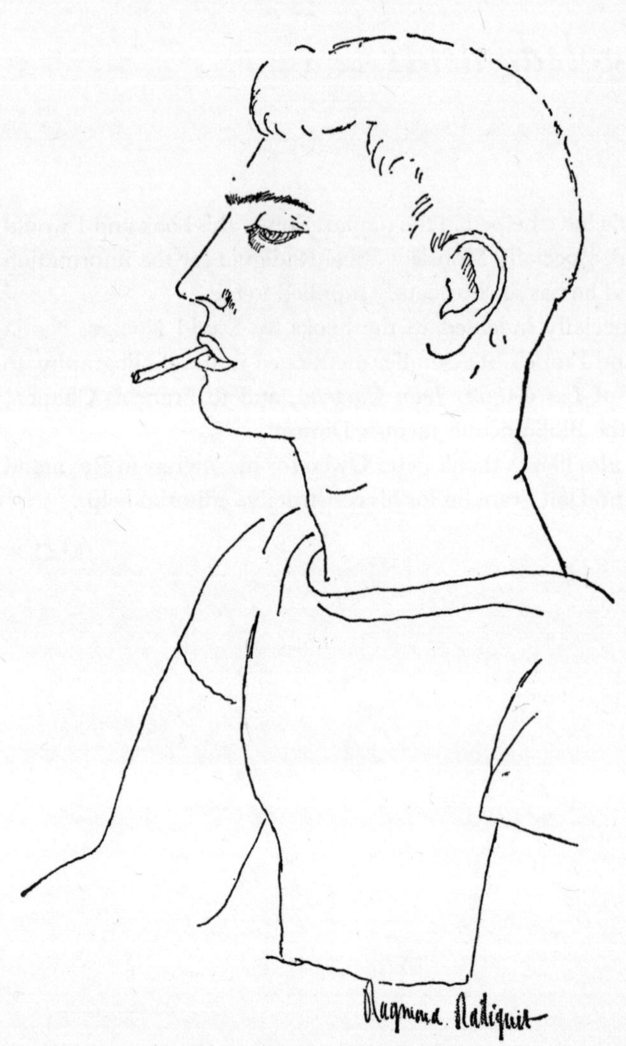

DRAWING BY JEAN COCTEAU

It is a commonplace, therefore true and not to be neglected, that one must live before one can write. But I would like to know at what age one has the right to say: 'I have lived.' Doesn't this use of the past tense imply, logically, death? I personally believe that at any age, and from the very beginning, one has both lived and is starting to live.

Raymond Radiguet

10 March, 1923

'Mon Premier Roman'
Les Nouvelles littéraires

F: *Avoir le diable au corps,* i) to be possessed, ii) to be full of devilment, iii) to be a tireless dancer.

Harrap's Standard French and English Dictionary, 1970

Introduction

Raymond Radiguet was born in June 1903 in an outer suburb of Paris and died in that city in December 1923. For about five years out of these twenty he wrote poems, articles, short stories and two novels, the second published only after his death. The first, *Le Diable au corps,* received a prize and became known in English as *The Devil in the Flesh.* The second, *Le Bal du comte d'Orgel,* is not as well known, perhaps because it is less melodramatic and more subtle, but its readership is increasing steadily.

No one today questions Radiguet's place in the development of the French novel. Now, a generation after his death, we know more about his life and his writing and it is possible to look more closely at his achievements. Speculation about his unfulfilled potential is tempting but dangerous and unrewarding. We see him now as a young man who grew up into a war – he was eleven in 1914 – dropped out of school and forced his way into journalism and literature. He accepted help, admiration and love from the many-talented Jean Cocteau but fought against domination by the older man through a series of liaisons with women who meant nothing to him. He failed to survive the pressures of early success in the crazy years that followed the war, dying from typhoid fever caught through eating oysters. Overwork and overplay had lowered his resistance. Cocteau maintained that Radiguet had anticipated his own death, and he mourned his young friend for the rest of his life.

Many photographs of Radiguet have survived and all offer a different face, for he was young and developing fast. This short study incorporates translations of some lesser-known prose writings on themes which vary as much as his own photographic image and shows how a schoolboy built his experience and his reading into work that made him not only professional but a classic before he was twenty-one. On the cards which his family sent to friends announcing his funeral, he was described as 'Monsieur Raymond Radiguet, *Homme de lettres*'.

M.C.

Starting to Live

Just after the First World War the poet Jean Cocteau was still light-hearted enough to describe his talented, unfathomable young friend Raymond Radiguet as 'the miracle of the Marne'. This may seem an odd joke to those who know their military history, but it was an obvious one. Radiguet was born close to this gentle river, at Parc Saint-Maur, a few miles to the east of Paris, and remained faithful to this district all his life. The visitor can sense the attraction of the river banks even today, despite the colourless suburban houses of the town. But Saint-Maur, set within a loop of the river, with its statue of Notre Dame des Miracles, has a personality of its own and keeps its natives close. With one exception all Radiguet's surviving brothers and sisters still live there.

Raymond Radiguet was born on 18 June, 1903 in one of these suburban houses, 30 *bis* avenue des Rochers. At eighteen his mother, Jeanne-Louise-Marie Tournier, who came from a Creole family apparently related to that of Joséphine de Beauharnais, had married Jules-Maurice Radiguet, eighteen years her senior, a successful artist, caricaturist and contributor to well-known newspapers and magazines including *l'Intransigeant* and the satiric, anticlerical, Anglophobe *Assiette au beurre.* His style of drawing was typical of the time, full of action, strongly satiric when necessary, essentially masculine. Examples of his work can be seen today at the Musée de l'Homme in Paris. There was a legend in his family that they were descended from the Poisson family whose most illustrious member had been Madame de Pompadour in the eighteenth century, but the unpretentious Radiguets did not take this story too seriously. Later on Cocteau was to make the most of it, writing a poem in which he made graceful complimentary references to both sides of his young friend's family.

Radiguet enjoyed his childhood: a happy one because so little happened. He later compared it to a flat lawn stretching as far as the eye could see. Yet every memorable episode, however slight, was recorded either by himself or by his friend Yves Krier who later became a journalist. Radiguet started school in a nursery class at the girls' school which his mother had left only a few years previously when she married; then, at the age of six, he entered the local *école communale,* the primary school. The young Raymond did well at school, although he hinted later that the reason was not brilliance but laziness – he did not muster the energy to rebel. He walked or ran to school with his younger brother René and they played in the old quarries which were a feature of the area. He may have been remembering his own parents when he wrote in his first novel that they loved him and did not scold him, but there seems to have been little opportunity for Radiguet to develop a close relationship with his mother. Radiguet was the eldest child, and she was constantly preoccupied with his younger brothers and sisters. In some autobiographical notes published after his death, one remark about his mother is particularly sad: he remembers that he never saw her face, she was always bending down to tie shoe-laces or otherwise help the younger children, three more boys and three girls. But he remembered her personality, and as a gentle, truly feminine woman she was to make discreet, idealized appearances in his work.

It was a happy, ordinary childhood in the house with its little garden and creaking gate. One of the earliest photographs of the young Radiguet shows him standing on a swing, wearing short trousers that look far too long and what appears to be a stiff white collar and a spotted cravat. From the age of about six he was fascinated by girls and later wrote about one of them in a narrative which originally formed the opening of his second novel, *Le Bal du comte d'Orgel.* Ever a realist, and fascinated by her plumpness, he said that she reminded him of a frog. 'Was it because I would often see her skipping with her legs apart, or because of her fat tummy; *beauty in children is lack of proportion.*' By the time he was twelve an attempted rendezvous with a little girl called Carmen had led to a confrontation with his teachers which he recounted, no doubt with extra colour, in *Le Diable au corps.* He involved his younger brother René with Carmen's sister Fauvette and René Radiguet remembers that the incident *did* occur, even the names of the two little girls remaining unchanged in the novel. There were other girls too, Yves Krier's sister and a young friend called Gertrude whom Radiguet declared to be his fiancée. However, for reasons best known to himself, he kept the arrangement secret from his prospective bride.

He was not so much obsessed with little girls as vastly curious, and his interest is only different from that felt by most boys because he felt it more deeply, remembered it and wrote about it. Did Radiguet's parents 'condemn' what the narrator in his novel calls '*la camaraderie mixte*'? If so they remained outwardly unconcerned and it was left to their son to note that 'sensuality, which is born with us and comes into being when still blind, gained from it instead of losing.'

In 1915, when he was twelve and due to leave his first school, Radiguet came top of the class and won the *Prix d'honneur.* Although his father was well paid for his work he was middle-aged now, still a free-lance artist bringing up a big family and he did not contemplate expensive education or training for his eldest son. Fortunately Raymond won a scholarship to the Lycée Charlemagne in Paris and for a year at least duly went there every day by omnibus or suburban train. The model schoolboy, however, was changing fast. Sometimes his parents noticed that he seemed remote from them, and there was a sad decline in his studies, proved by the details from his school records which were published by Keith Goesch in 1955. 'Is it my fault,' says the narrator of *Le Diable au corps,* 'that I had my twelfth birthday a few months before the declaration of war?' A war which comes to one's gate is hardly a good background for study and again, if the narrator were remembering actual events, it even looks as if the family contemplated flight from Saint-Maur, by bicycle.

During the autumn term of 1916 he had studied ten subjects, earning zero for drawing, as though to annoy his father, and remaining practically at the bottom of the class in Greek, mathematics and natural history. In French and Latin he did better, but by the following year he had dropped half-way down the class in both subjects and given up all the others. His disappointed father discovered that he was playing truant, leaving the house in the morning but not going to the Lycée. Raymond was in fact spending happy hours in his father's boat on the Marne, mostly reading, sometimes even writing. A few years later he described, again in his first novel, what the war years were like for someone of his age – four years of holiday.

Unfortunately his father considered he was reading too many of the wrong authors – Rimbaud and Verlaine for example, who were certainly not taught in French lycées at the time – and even magazines or books of poems by young or avant-garde writers. Maurice Radiguet believed his son's education to be important and, busy though he was, decided to supervise it himself. He tried to make him study a variety of subjects at home but the boy remained fiercely obstinate. Raymond read the French classics, borrowing the books from him and taking them out to the boat, but that was all.

There was another probable reason for his lack of interest in school work and ironically enough his father may unwittingly have been the cause of it. In the spring of 1917 Radiguet saw him talking to a young woman on the platform of an omnibus on the way to Paris. She was a local teacher named Alice, whose husband Gaston had been called up. She missed him, and with time on her hands she wanted to arrange an exhibition of the watercolours that she painted as a hobby. Maurice Radiguet was obviously well placed to help her. Soon, however, she seems to have found his eldest son more interesting than anyone or anything else. The two young people – the boy of fourteen and the woman of twenty-four – were often seen together in the neighbourhood and when they wanted to escape they went rowing on the Marne.

What happened between them? Alice was apparently not attractive in any obvious way, she was thin, with 'a long nose, quivering nostrils and an intense gaze with a gleam of exaltation'. Radiguet had already shown strong interest in small girls and his curiosity had a more intensely sexual motivation now. This relationship was not openly discussed in France until thirty years after Radiguet's death; it was obviously the starting point of his first novel, but probably no more than that. Radiguet did not start writing *Le Diable au corps* until two years later and took two more years to complete it, by which time his experience was wider and deeper. Raymond soon tired of Alice, but she did not give him up so easily. She and her husband did not disappear from his life and were to make a dramatic return later. But during 1917, while the 'holiday' of the war years still lasted, Radiguet's life became suddenly so full, intense and creative in other ways that the dubious glamour of a suburban love affair faded as quickly as it had flared.

Again his father took a hand in the boy's destiny, again unwittingly. He needed a messenger to take his drawings into the city and his son was the obvious choice. Raymond welcomed any chance to go into Paris and particularly into editors' offices, for, stimulated by his reading of literary magazines, he had begun to write poems and short stories. Early in 1918, before he was fifteen, he saw himself in print for the first time, unexpectedly in the satiric daily paper *Le Canard enchaîné,* then only three years old. The little piece was called *Galanterie française* and was signed with the pseudonym 'Rajky'. Perhaps Radiguet thought the name sounded amusing or exotic, or perhaps his editor had suggested it. No one has yet explained how the piece was accepted and published but no others followed in the same paper. However, the messenger boy wasted no time. He was noticed by André Salmon, editor of *L'Intransigeant,* for whom Maurice Radiguet contributed a daily cartoon for the front page. Salmon was a poet, not merely an editor; the memoirs he wrote later, and his biography of Modigliani have become well known. He remembered the first appearance in his office of the boy who still wore short trousers and the uncomfortable stiff collar which teenage boys could hardly escape. He remembered too, no doubt with hindsight, details more telling than clothes; he referred to the 'nice little boy with the sharp gaze of an adult who was still naïve but very likely to become cruel; yes, a strange gaze darkened by a rebellious lock of hair hanging in heavy folds, like the hard vizor of a helmet.'

Radiguet's 'cruelty' was to emerge later. For the time being he knew that he would have to push his way into print. Publishing of all kinds was restricted by the war, there was nobody to lobby for him, his father would have preferred him to study and most people still treated him as a schoolboy. He was prepared to do anything to attract attention. He told André Salmon that his father was not the only artist in the family, he made drawings himself. Also, he wrote poems and would be glad to see them published.

Salmon looked at his poems, and later professed to have been impressed by their 'exquisite sobriety', advising him to be himself and not to hide behind some improbable, mythical creature called Rajky. During the second half of 1918, when Radiguet was fifteen, three of his poems appeared in the literary magazine *Sic* which was edited by Pierre-Albert Birot; the first, at least, was signed 'Raimon Rajky'. They were written in the avant-garde language of the moment and tried to achieve an effect through eccentric layout with many blank spaces and no capital letters or punctuation. He had obviously been influenced by Apollinaire and by many lesser poets of the time. By now these poems are merely curiosities in the history of a literary personality and can hardly be read for pleasure. They certainly provided none for Apollinaire himself in the last year of his life: he accused Radiguet of plagiarism. However, he told him not to despair; Rimbaud, he said, had not written his masterpiece until he was nineteen.

POEM

a red eiderdown at the window
flowers in   the under-
pants crutch   that warm garden in the wallflower
scent of warm dried clothes
the chestnut tree sings
would it be   those pink candles set in irregular
pattern or else   a   bird
on th   l ne the cl th s d n e
e i   o   e   a   c

e   e sh t   h   t   a   t
on   arm d   ir   t   a   w   n   s

t em   e m
o   b r a c   e

Raimon Rajky
Sic, 1918

Radiguet grew up within the space of a few months. Having seen a little of his work in print he now wanted much more than sporadic publication, he wanted a literary career, money of his own and independence from home. From poems and short prose pieces he progressed rapidly to commercial journalism, especially when Salmon found him an opening with a paper called *L'Heure*. He also contributed to *L'Eveil* and for six months was even editorial secretary to the well-known humorous journal *Le Rire*. Many of his colleagues were jealous of him, saying that since he had no experience he did not deserve to be paid for his journalistic efforts. But at fifteen and sixteen Radiguet's personality was so well-developed that somehow or other he would always get his own way. The distinguished Doctor Roux of the Institut Pasteur refused to be interviewed by the apparent schoolboy who came to see him, but without much effort the 'schoolboy' won him over and the interview was given. Another story about Radiguet at this confused period of his life is that he immediately began to frequent the Café du Croissant in the rue du Croissant, near the Gare du Nord, a well-known rendezvous for professional journalists. It had been notorious in 1914 for a time because Jean Jaurès, the socialist leader, was shot there just before the outbreak of war. Radiguet persuaded his older colleagues to play belote with him and had no trouble in beating them. They would even listen to Alice when she came to look for him. Radiguet also persuaded the management to give him credit. According to one of his French biographers, Clément Borgal, 'an astonishing firmness allowed him to achieve almost immediately what he had decided upon. Insolent, shy, naïve and calculating in turn, more or less unfathomable', he would immediately dominate the scene, and the same thing happened in 'social life, love or literature'.

Little of social life or love crept into his early poems, but there was plenty of attempted literature. These poems must have seemed right for the literary reviews in which they appeared, reviews that reflected the chaos of the war and the years that immediately followed. If the adult world appears confusing to any teenager, the atmosphere of literary Paris in 1918 must have seemed doubly so, for amidst the chaos and confusion of the war had sprung up new ventures, full of exciting, creative potential. In spite of the fighting and the heavy loss of life there had been no diminution in literary activity. New reviews had appeared, one after the other: Francis Picabia's *391* in 1915, *Sic* the following year, Pierre Reverdy's *Nord-Sud* in 1917, while the last year of the war brought Tristan Tzara's Dadaist manifesto and all the argument that surrounded it. *Littérature,* edited by André Breton and Louis Aragon, was to follow in 1919. Radiguet obviously followed all this avant-garde activity and at the same time succeeded in meeting some older writers. He encountered such varied figures as Max Jacob, Blaise Cendrars, Breton, and Aragon. As Cocteau was to remark later, these were Radiguet's 'classics'.

Cocteau: the name always so closely associated with that of Radiguet that the younger man has been sometimes misunderstood and misrepresented. In 1919 Jean Cocteau was thirty, for ten years he had been publishing poetry and critical manifestoes blazoning his own activities and those of his avant-garde friends, not only writers but painters and composers too. He had published drawings, devised ballets and with Cendrars he had founded a small publishing firm. He had been to the western front with an ambulance unit, wearing a kind of fancy dress uniform. He shared his mother's apartment on the Right Bank and appeared equally at home among the aristocracy, the *haute bourgeoisie* or the avant-garde. He was omnipresent, always talked about, the centre of a wide circle of friends, men and women, and irresistibly pederastic. It is hard now to believe there was a time when Cocteau and Radiguet did not know each other and it is not surprising that several people have taken the credit for introducing them. André Salmon claims he sent the boy to see Max Jacob, the Jew from Brittany now aged forty-three, well known for his prose poems, his homosexuality and also for his conversion to Christianity. He must have won Radiguet's confidence quickly for the boy who was so often shy and stubborn was calling him *'tu'* within a week. Either Salmon or Jacob introduced Radiguet to Cocteau. According to Cocteau himself his first sight of the boy was in 1918 in a picture gallery. But as Cocteau admitted himself, he had a tendency to confuse dates, and most of his friends recall the occasion as being in 1919. It was Radiguet's first appearance in the literary world and Cocteau was certainly present. 'I saw then for the first time,' wrote Jean Hugo in his journal for 1919, 'a personage whose few steps on this earth were to leave a profound impression. During a warm afternoon in June the memory of Apollinaire was being celebrated at the Galerie Léonce Rosenberg in the rue de la Baume. Poets read some poems and pages of prose by the poet who died on the last day of the war. Shortly before the end of the session an unknown person came through the crowd of spectators on his way to the platform. Above a long, thick, beaver-coloured flannel coat, in which he seemed to have spent the night, emerged the waxen face of a child; his eyebrows were joined together above his pale, almost sightless eyes, his tousled hair fell onto the coat collar, his mouth with its very full lips was grave. After he had read his page he went through the room again, unmoved and as though walking in the dark. It was Raymond Radiguet.' According to others present Cocteau did not appear to pay any particular attention to him on this occasion.

Shortly afterwards, however, Radiguet came to the Cocteau apartment in the rue d'Anjou. Cocteau was to write a famous description of this meeting. The valet told him that 'a child with a walking stick' had called and asked to see him. Perhaps Radiguet thought he would look a little older if he carried a cane – it can be seen in one of Jacques-Emile Blanche's portraits of him and in photographs taken later. If Radiguet really looked as Cocteau described him then he would have attracted attention anywhere. Cocteau insisted that he at once realized his 'star-quality', although it was hardly obvious. 'He was small, pale, short-sighted, his badly cut hair hung over his collar and gave him side-whiskers. He screwed up his face as though the sun was in his eyes. He skipped as he walked. For him pavements seemed to have been made of rubber. He would pull little sheets of copy-book paper out of his pockets, rolled up into balls. He would flatten them out with his hand . . . and try to read a very short poem.' He rolled his own cigarettes, and they would get in his way as he read. If he had no spectacles with him he would hold the poems up to his eyes, sometimes using broken spectacles like a monocle.

Although Cocteau also wrote that he met Radiguet at Jacob's place, there were other contenders for the role of go-between. Radiguet, after all, had met other, older people, writers and painters. André Breton has told how one day he and Radiguet were walking across the Place de la Concorde when they met Cocteau. Breton realized at once that his two acquaintances would surely plunge into an *amitié particulière,* a 'special friendship', homosexual love. He was aware of a 'current of electricity' between the two men, and since there have been many accounts of how Cocteau fell in love, intensely and often, sometimes at first sight, Breton's phrase has a ring of truth.

Radiguet's personal relationships, especially during 1919, when he was fiercely preoccupied with furthering his career, could hardly avoid complication. No sooner had he met Breton and his friends than he began to make enemies, a fact he was even ready to advertise. In the summer of that year he wrote to Breton hoping that they would meet on a certain occasion. He went on: 'And I hope I don't meet Louis Aragon who has the power of irritating me intensely – very likeable apart from that and other things. And to think that everyone makes you responsible for the words, deeds and gestures (they are numerous) of this PUPPET. His strings could be of better quality.'

But Radiguet was still schoolboy enough to change his opinions abruptly; perhaps too he hardly knew what went on in his own mind, at least as far as friendship was concerned. Just over a month later he wrote again, wondering if Breton was angry with him, asking him to accept his apologies and adding that this was not a move to ingratiate himself and secure publication in *Littérature.* It looks as though Breton had attempted some kind of mediation for in his next letter Radiguet said he would write to Aragon, that Breton's suggestion was excellent. 'What I said to you about him doesn't count, you know that anyway: what one says never counts. (I love people like him, who have talent. You only have to read one of his poems to see that this is his *métier.*)' During 1919 Radiguet published three poems and a *chronique* in *Littérature* but he never had a genuine change of heart about Aragon, as a note to some critical writing, *Règle du jeu,* was to show the following year.

His friendship with Tristan Tzara, founder of Dada, seems to have been genuine, if brief. He published a *poème scénique* in the Dada anthology of 1919 and was probably drawn to Dada in the hope of entering the literary scene, for he did not care how he did so. His early poems are too self-conscious to rank as genuine Dada material, and it was kind-hearted of Tzara to accept them. He even asked Radiguet on one occasion to 'explain' one poem, hardly typical in Dada circles, surely. Radiguet soon moved on.

He was ambitious and, as far as his work was concerned, unscrupulous. Apart from his family, whom he genuinely loved, he probably never cared deeply for anyone, but at this point he needed people. Obviously he responded to Cocteau as a friend, probably as a lover, but for his work he needed most of all the older man's guidance, his gift for talent-spotting and for acting as go-between with editors and publishers. The cynical interpretation would be that he saw more future and more entertainment with Cocteau, who had friends in all the arts and most coteries, than with the over-cerebral surrealists led by the despotic André Breton. He encountered surrealism at a moment when he was developing too fast to become involved in a movement which limited freedom even while advocating freedom before anything else. Cocteau seemed to represent total freedom, for in spite of all his friends and hangers-on he was too much of an individual to register outside influences for long. He was also the most professional of all amateurs, unconcerned with family problems (apart from his dominating mother) or money worries.

In the early autumn of 1919 Cocteau was away from Paris for several weeks, staying with the composer Louis Durey in a Basque village, but despite his physical absence he obviously felt himself coming closer to Radiguet. He wrote to him regularly, wished they were together, and complained that he did not receive many answers to his letters. But some of Radiguet's too rare replies contained poems and these delighted Cocteau. Before he even called his new friend *tu* he referred to him as an adopted son and advised him to wear proper spectacles. He urged him to stay at home and write. Cocteau was already becoming possessive: he knew how attractive his protégé was to both sexes and feared that if he spent too much time in Montmartre or Montparnasse he would soon attract other admirers.

Inevitably Radiguet was drawn closely into the life that had developed round Cocteau – theatre visits of all kinds, and concerts, especially where modern music was played, including the strange works of Erik Satie and the mainly light-hearted compositions by the group later known as *Les Six* (Georges Auric, Honegger, Milhaud, Poulenc, Germaine Tailleferre and, for a time at least, Durey). Radiguet began to come to the rue d'Anjou regularly and often wrote at Cocteau's desk, which did not please Madame Cocteau. She thought him untidy and, after all, he came from a different class. Cocteau, who soon found his company essential, took him everywhere, to exhibitions and to artists' studios. Although Radiguet took his friend to Saint-Maur and introduced him to his family, he was at home less and less. After long evenings in cafés and bars he would sometimes take the last train back home, or walk back through the Bois de Vincennes, hoping the lions would not roar and frighten him, but more often he would stay in the city. If he missed the train, 'He would go back, either to Montmartre or Montparnasse and sleep in someone's studio, anywhere, among the canvases, tubes of paint or easels.' Cocteau had introduced him to the artists Jean and Valentine Hugo, and when he slept on the divan in their dining-room a lithograph of Shelley would watch over him.

René Radiguet remembers that even when preoccupied with his new exciting life in Paris his brother Raymond would nearly always come home on Sundays to spend the day with his family. His father, essentially a family man and aware of his continuing responsibilities, began to feel anxious about his eldest son. He suspected Cocteau's influence and even wrote to him, particularly after he had found letters which seemed to indicate that the two men were arranging assignations in a well-known Paris hotel. The poet replied firmly to Monsieur Radiguet urging him to have confidence in him, and to do what he could – and should – to improve his son's health. The boy needed plenty of exercise, food and sleep, he told him. He pointed out that (through him) Raymond was now being paid by Jacques Doucet, the rich couturier-collector, for short manuscript articles, and inferred that the secretary to Lord Derby, the British Ambassador, had invited him to luncheon and found him charming. Cocteau had hoped that this might lead to the offer of a job.

Radiguet's meeting with Jacques Doucet was in fact profitable in more ways than one, for he could be certain thereafter of payment whenever he sent the collector a manuscript and he was free to write what he wished. Radiguet's letters to Monsieur Doucet were excessively polite. He thanked his Maecenas for a pair of gloves, told him he would write critical articles only about books that he liked (an attitude he had probably learnt from Cocteau but did not keep) and gave his opinion of Reverdy's latest book, saying that what he had read he found 'particularly curious as proof of his pride and his irascible character'.

By December 1919, just after Cocteau had replied to his father's letter of complaint, Radiguet gave Doucet some important news. 'I'm sending you an article by the same post, it's rather short, for at the moment I'm working on a novel. I'm really glad to do these articles for you, since it makes me interested in writing prose, which is very useful. So if by chance my first novel were interesting, it's you I should thank, for you gave me the idea of writing in prose.' Apart from a few prose poems, the only prose he had published so far had been an article about the painter Juan Gris and a second, in *Littérature,* about another painter, Irène Lagut.

Radiguet was full of contradictions, sometimes stubbornly, rudely silent, sometimes, according to the British painter Nina Hamnett, exquisitely polite. Both attitudes showed him to be remote, anxious to make contacts, if not friends, but equally anxious not to reveal any feeling of insecurity. He was resentfully aware that he was already something of a prodigy and he hated the idea. Nowadays, half a century later, young writers are accepted as normal, if exceptional. But Radiguet had only the example of the mysterious Rimbaud to live up to – and that was challenge enough. His contemporaries noted a strange mixture of shyness and what could only be called arrogance, even cruelty. He was so determined to be adult, mature – and to achieve this maturity overnight – that he adopted intransigent attitudes towards anything that struck him as less than first-rate. He was too young to be sympathetic and understanding of other people's problems; he had too many of his own. Cocteau has recounted how his young friend reacted in an artist's studio when shown a painting that was 'not quite finished'. Radiguet gave it a cold look. 'It would be humane,' he said, 'to finish it off.'

Several of the people who knew him have remarked on the streak of cruelty that seemed to be embedded in his nature. Probably it was due to an excess of mental energy that demanded an outlet, and to envy. Radiguet envied anyone with literary success, the success he wanted but could not find until he had come to terms with life. Nevertheless, he had come a long way. It was far enough, at the age of sixteen, from Parc Saint-Maur to the rue d'Anjou and the cafés of Montmartre and Montparnasse, but he sensed he had still further to go. In the meantime he could find the courage to write polite letters to his patron and he knew the art of the 'casual' offer, offering the only thing he possessed, his talent.

In that December letter to Doucet Radiguet showed that he possessed at least sufficient confidence to ask for money, and he did so, very politely, and giving an irresistible reason: 'There is one thing I prefer to ask you by letter, rather than in person. For the New Year I would like to give certain ladies I know [*certaines personnes de mes amies*] some flowers or sweets. And I have at home one of my manuscripts decorated with watercolours, ten or twelve recent poems which are the sequel to the manuscripts you possess.

'I admit that asking you this embarrasses me greatly, without any reason, moreover. . . .'

He was probably referring to a work which can be seen today in the Doucet collection in Paris: poems written out carefully, but certainly not in copperplate hand, edged with watercolour drawings of flowers – poppies, nasturtiums and gladioli. There are also ladies wearing crinolines and carrying sunshades, and on one page a small child looking through binoculars and a solitary young man sitting in a park, reading. Radiguet was no draughtsman, but the arrangement of the motifs on the pages and the delicate colouring have a kind of girlish charm.

There was nothing else girlish about him, and when he wrote this letter to Jacques Doucet he was writing poems which show how often and how intensely he noticed girls, their white dresses and flowery hats. These creatures also featured in the prose which Doucet and Cocteau encouraged him to write. If he really was working at a novel already, he was probably planning the two early episodes in *Le Diable au corps,* the anecdote about the two little girls, Carmen and Fauvette, and the grisly story about the maid-servant who went mad and threw herself off the roof of the neighbouring house in Parc Saint-Maur, a true story apparently, and one that had made a deep impression on the schoolboy Radiguet.

He may even have been writing the first draft of an account of his love affair with Alice; in this early version she is called 'Alice' and is married to a naval officer. Its tone is bitter and full of a wish for revenge, as though Radiguet had been deeply hurt by his first love affair. Alice asks him to post a letter to her husband, and then: '(did she know I would not resist the pain of opening it?) I saw those words of love with which she soothed me, those diminutives, ridiculous when you think of them in cold blood, were the same for him.' The relationship is destroyed. These pages probably show the nature of the experience Radiguet was living through, and, more important, how he reacted. 'From this first love I no doubt emerged transformed, but not in the way I thought. I didn't come out of it "a man", I came out of it "old".' And he wished Alice dead.

1920

At the start of 1920, however, Radiguet was not 'old', he was sixteen and a half; he had published poems typical of the times, written a few polite letters to his patron and at least one to Cocteau which ended '*Je vous adore*'. However impressionable he might have been, he fortunately carried a schoolboy sense of humour into adolescence and beyond. He could not resist writing parodies of his favourite writers. Totally absurd, and fortunately brief, is the revue sketch *Hommage à Chateaubriand,* written early in 1920 but unpublished until 1955. Imagine a chorus of ten bears, and their leader, a polar bear, announcing to the romantic hero, a 'Pale Young Man', that they are drunk. There are jokes and puns about honey and honeymoons and a lyric by the Pale Young Man with an amusing stanza:

Mieux que dans les feéries
Si je joue au bilboquet
Lune il faut vous résigner
Une abeille me piquait
Sur ma lèvre chagrinée
Et qui ne voulait pas mourir
Se transformait en sourire

Radiguet later wrote another poem about the *bilboquet* (a cup-and-ball), a toy which obviously intrigued him, and is evidently a sexual symbol, one of the many which recur to an obsessional degree in Radiguet's poetry.

In April 1920, when he was nearly seventeen, he indicated grandly to Jacques Doucet that he was now in a position to see recent literature in perspective: 'So many things have happened in the literary world that I'll enjoy writing for you what I think about Dada and so-called "cubist literature".' (His curt remarks about Max Jacob, Blaise Cendrars and Pierre Reverdy, entitled *'Notes secrètes sur quelques poètes "cubistes"'* do not appear to have been published before 1955). Apollinaire's work, he wrote, was 'worthy of the most severe classical anthologies'; Jacob had introduced a new sensitivity but needed self-control; while 'Today young people are amazed that they once admired Reverdy.' He could hardly have accused *himself* of that: he never missed an opportunity to attack Reverdy, a poet whose reputation has in fact continued to grow since his death.

Radiguet was more than ever determined to grow up quickly – instantly, in fact. However precarious his relationship with Breton and Aragon during the first few months of 1920, his poems were still being published in *Littérature,* and he continued to write short prose pieces and reviews, including one of Cocteau's ballet *Le Boeuf sur le toit* which had been performed at the Comédie des Champs-Elysées in February. Radiguet has been credited with a share in devising this 'farce', as Cocteau called it, which has become identified with the 'twenties in Paris, but his name was never attached to it.

His visits to the theatre filled him with ideas. The more plays and ballets he saw the more he wanted to write for the stage. He managed to put his ideas down on paper and eagerly showed them to his friends. 'Have you read *Les Pélican*?' he asked Monsieur Doucet in May 1920. This was a play in two acts, the only piece of dramatic writing included in the Grasset edition of the *Oeuvres complètes.* It was a literary joke, funny enough to be performed the following year and still funny in 1951 when it was revived. It was a literary joke for those who like theatrical nonsense, but Radiguet took his jokes seriously, for he wanted people to take *him* seriously.

Monsieur and Madame Pélican have a son Anselme and a daughter Hortense. Monsieur loves their governess, Mademoiselle Charmant, but she is borne away by the valet de chambre, Parfait, in a suitcase. Madame Pélican is adored by Monsieur Pastel, her swimming instructor. Pélican protests when Anselme says he wants to be a jockey and Hortense a gardener. When their father points out that the family name is famous and mentions the romantic poet Alfred de Musset, Hortense recites thirty-three of his most famous lines from *La Nuit de Mai: 'Lorsque le pélican, lassé d'un long voyage. . . .'* It is decided that Anselme will be a poet and Hortense a photographer. She falls in love with her teacher Monsieur Chantecler and says she will drown herself. Since the Seine is frozen she wins a skating competition instead. Anselme announces that he has lost enough weight to become a jockey. Hortense wants a family photograph and, as she insists on being included, Monsieur Pastel (who incidentally cannot swim) takes it. *Les Pélican* includes other jokes and even references to some of Radiguet's own poems.

There is no record of what Monsieur Doucet thought of the play. It is funnier than a short summary can suggest, owing something to the American comedy films that the author and his friends enjoyed at the time. It also shares something with *Le Boeuf sur le toit* and with one of Cocteau's most amusing and influential works, *Les Mariés de la Tour Eiffel,* which was written during the same year and like Radiguet's play was performed during 1921. Radiguet loved farce and enjoyed himself by including crazy episodes: Mademoiselle Charmant has been reading *La Vie parisienne* in secret and since she has fallen out of her hammock she may in fact be dead; Hortense removes flowers from her mother's hats and plants them in the billiard table. The theatre of the absurd does not seem very far away.

This kind of writing, like Cocteau's work at the same period, reflected the mood of many younger writers in France two or three years after the end of the war. Selfishly, they were determined to forget the war and its horrors. Indeed Cocteau and Radiguet had little reason for forgetfulness: the war had been a holiday for Radiguet and a ludicrous adventure for Cocteau. The music of Cocteau's composer friends was usually light-hearted and full of new rhythms from both North and South America. At this moment no one in Cocteau's immediate circle was concerned with social change. They left such earnest preoccupations to other writers, such as Henri Barbusse, who had published his famous war novel *Le Feu* back in 1916 and was now preaching communist ideals. Breton and his followers also began to turn towards Moscow, perhaps because the French socialists had lacked a convincing leader since the assassination of Jaurès in 1914.

To the general public the aftermath of the war seemed as bad as, if not worse than, the war itself – a situation which occurred again in 1945. Those who had hoped for good times after the armistice were disappointed: in Paris all places where music and dancing took place had to close at eleven p.m. by law, to save electricity. There were clandestine night clubs, hundreds of them, usually lit by candles or paraffin lamps and run by unscrupulous men like Desmond in Colette's *The Last of Chéri.* But they were expensive and no substitute for the good old days – Chéri himself, when he leaves the army, finds Paris so changed that he no longer sees any point in living, and shoots himself.

But other young men were not so aggressive in their disillusionment and found ways of enjoying themselves. Cocteau was to write later that people had forgotten how to play, but he and his circle of friends had not and this was demonstrated at those famous Saturday dinners that he and so many others have described so well. Here is Cocteau's description in *Le Rappel à l'ordre*: 'This weekly dinner took place in 1919-20-21, either at Montmartre, or Place de la Madeleine. We organized it, I and the musicians, in order to meet at fixed times. Later, these dinners developed into a wider kind of reunion. We never talked about art. We used to go, after dinner, to Milhaud's rooms, who at that time was composing *Le Boeuf sur le toit,* and would play it with Auric and Arthur Rubinstein, arranged for six hands. Paul Morand and Lucien Daudet were the barmen. Morand carried ice about in a napkin, and it used to melt and numb our hands. When there was no more left, he would shake up the last drinks with the help of snow scraped up from the window-sill. We disguised ourselves, and rode a bicycle round the tiny dining-room – in short, did everything which sounds appalling when talked about afterwards, but which at the time is far more stimulating to everyone in his own sphere than the literary café.'

The dinners in fact took place in many different restaurants all over Paris, and afterwards the *convives,* the 'Mutual Admiration

Society', as Paul Morand called them, would go back to someone's room or out into the streets, or to a fairground where they would be photographed in one of those exotic, painted frames which usually produce a highly comic effect. There is such a photograph of Radiguet, his face topped by an absurd toreador's hat. It is one of the very few in which he seems utterly happy.

He had a capacity for enjoyment and a definite sense of humour. He was still young enough to find a good deal of satisfaction in purely literary jokes like his *Hommage à Chateaubriand* or *Les Pélican,* but at the same time believed himself practical and in touch with everyday life. He admitted that he enjoyed reading the newspapers, as though this was something of a vice, and loftily quoted Goethe's example: 'Let us not lose interest in our own age.' He also read them, as any potential fiction writer does, to find hints for plots, or continual proof that nature imitates art.

Literature was almost all he knew about: the classics he had read at school or at home, and the work being written around him. 'On one side,' wrote Cocteau, 'there was the dreariest kind of conventionality and on the other a remarkable chaos made up of all kinds of experimental work. These daring experiments, like tongues of fire, or alcohol-burning flames which spurted through the smallest cracks and devoured everything (and each other at the same time), were Radiguet's classics. He learned to read among the extremes.' Or, as Cocteau later stated, he and his friends, 'we were his classics'. Radiguet learned from them and soon moved on from the experimental chaos of his early poems to literary games. (Still little more than a schoolboy, *he* had not 'forgotten how to play'.) Yet even while playing games Radiguet had something to say. Beneath the absurd surface of *Les Pélican* is a serious theme that reoccurs in so much of his work: young people refusing to do what their parents expected of them. Anselme and Hortense are cheerful, harmless young people with no grudge against society, but they still make a bid for unorthodox careers. The theme is now familiar – in life as well as literature – but it was less so then, just as the boy who 'drops out' of school is a familiar figure today. When Radiguet made his protest at the age of twelve he was more of a unique phenomenon.

No wonder he did not want to be young, for there was no particular merit in youth in the early 1920s. And he had rebelled at an early age, sacrificing the last years of childhood to his literary ambitions. These ambitions drove him still, and they confused his personal relationships. He was dependent on acquiring yet more friends and at the same time saw himself becoming dangerously dependent on Cocteau. He knew he was still experimenting with living as he was with writing. Cocteau loved him, *he* did not love Cocteau, but it was too early yet to make the experiment of rejecting him. And he obviously realized that so far he had borrowed more from Cocteau than the older man would ever admit.

In the meantime Jean Cocteau had decided to start yet another literary magazine, *Le Coq,* for all the existing ones attacked him, usually for the wrong reasons, and none of them had provided a suitable platform for himself and his many friends. He felt more confident now, his group was acquiring an odd kind of power, and he was reasonably experienced in magazine publication – he had edited *Schéhérazade* as far back as 1908 with his friend François Bernouard as printer and just at the beginning of the war he and Paul Iribe had edited *Le Mot,* one of the reviews that Radiguet used to read when he was playing truant from the Lycée. After his journalistic experience under Salmon's guidance Radiguet was able to contribute in a semi-professional way to the running of the magazine. Although the first number contained a poem by Cocteau and an article about Schoenberg it was the piece by Radiguet that caught the reader's attention, a plea for 'ordinary' straightforward writing, painting and music. How quickly he had worked his way through the '-isms'! 'Musset created his work,' he wrote, 'without thinking about romanticism. In the same way Jean Cocteau writes without aiming at modernism.' He naturally praised his friend, who had written an editorial in the same straightforward vein. 'There is so much novelty in him that he can allow himself to breathe in the scent of a rose.' Cocteau in fact insisted, in this first number, on the 'disappearance of the skyscraper' and the 'reappearance of the rose'. Radiguet's text, entitled 'Since 1789 they've been forcing me to think', takes up a phrase he had used in a letter written to Cocteau the previous year. The two men were obviously working side by side and Cocteau was to insist later that Radiguet was his 'teacher'. For the moment, however, Radiguet was learning, very fast.

The second number of *Le Coq,* prepared by Radiguet while Cocteau was in England, came out in June, publishing work by Erik Satie and three members of *Les Six,* while the list of contributors included Paul Morand, the future novelist, then in the diplomatic service, and Cocteau's friend Lucien Daudet. Radiguet himself, who was seventeen this month, contributed a short prose poem called *Halte!,* addressed to a girl cyclist in a trouser skirt, and a short story, an anecdote, entitled *La Marchande de fleurs (The Flower-Girl).*

THE FLOWER-GIRL

No one has forgotten the mysterious circumstances in which a swan was stolen from the zoological gardens. The *chansonniers* hinted that this theft was a consequence of the price of poultry. A socialist deputy took advantage of it to attack the government. But the public refused to believe that such an unusual theft did not have an extraordinary motive.

The keepers at the zoo were well acquainted with little Aline, the flower-girl, who, on the days when generous clients had relieved her of her violets and mimosa, would run to one of those multi-coloured kiosks which are a children's paradise.

Aline did not distribute casually the bread rolls with which she filled her apron. She would willingly have shared her picnic dinner with her favourite swan, but the selfish creature did not invite her. As soon as the flower-seller's apron was empty the unusual favourite took his leave of the naïve young girl.

This behaviour on the part of such a majestic animal would have surprised anyone who has not read the tales of chivalry, in which fine ladies can be seen entertaining gentlemen.

Aline lived on the sixth floor of a not very respectable hotel. Her exemplary conduct caused surprise among the neighbouring girls:

'At her age,' they would say, 'at fourteen, we weren't selling flowers any longer.'

On Aline's bedroom wall hung a coloured print showing the seduction of Leda by Jupiter. Unaware as she was of the ancient fable and seeing in Leda only a rival, she became indignant:

'How ungrateful of him!'

One thundery evening she tore down the print. The next day she thought she could detect a look of reproach in the eyes of her swan.

'Why are you jealous? My romance with Leda is already ancient history.'

It had become fashionable again to wear a flower in one's buttonhole. Aline became rich very, very quickly. She rented a comfortable apartment in a pleasant district.

Aline now earned enough money for two people. She wrote to the director of the zoological gardens and suggested she might buy the swan. But postmen are so absent-minded that she received no reply.

She had always been honest. So her heart beat very fast when, at the time the keepers close the gates, she abducted her beloved. Since he was very intelligent he took care not to sing, knowing that Aline did not want him to die. . . .

They arrived without difficulty at the entrance to her apartment. The swan was installed in the bathtub. And the girl no longer needed to envy children of her age who play with a swan in the bath. Only hers was not made of celluloid.

* * *

The Flower-Girl might seem fragile, but Radiguet had worked hard on it. This is the second version, shorter apparently than the original draft. Although many of his poems show him preoccupied with classical mythology this was one of the rare occasions it strayed into his prose. Here of course he is trying hard to produce a sophisticated, cynical smile. Did he by any chance remember a phrase in one of the letters Cocteau had written to him the previous year, when he felt close to his own childhood again: 'I'm back with my celluloid duck in the bathtub'?

The swan motif occurs fairly often in Radiguet's poetry, and at certain periods Cocteau used it frequently too, especially when he could make a mysterious pun on the words *cygne* (swan) and *signe* (sign).

Cocteau's magazine continued for only two more numbers, for which it was called *Le Coq parisien.* The late summer issue concentrated on a 'celebration' of the painter Douanier Rousseau, printing in three colours a folding supplement which could be opened out. The only contributions from Radiguet were a short notice about *Le Journal quotidien* and a short poem, *Prise d'armes,* which for some reason was left unsigned. At the same time came Radiguet's most solid achievement to date when François Bernouard published *Les Joues en feu,* a collection of fourteen poems, at the end of July. The plaquette, without pagination, was embellished with four drypoints by Jean Hugo. Radiguet hastened to give Jacques Doucet a copy, one of those printed on India paper; he would have given him the first of the numbered copies, but unfortunately, he wrote, there was a hole in the paper.

The poems were infinitely better than the incoherent scraps, now discarded, that had first brought his name into print. Those he selected for this publication had acquired individuality and a certain amount of depth. If their images still seem detached and isolated they at least remain in the mind and allow the reader to interpret them as he wishes.

The author wrote no preface to his poems – there were too few of them and he was too close to them – but he later wrote a valuable introduction to the revised collection which was eventually published in 1925, two years after his death. 'My poems,' he said, 'are the natural expression of a mixture of *pudeur* and secretiveness suited to the age at which they were written.' He added that he had been more influenced by the classics – Ronsard, Chénier, Malherbe, La Fontaine, Tristan L'Hermite – than by anyone else. He 'confessed' that the most interesting aspect of a poet's production was psychological and his poems could perhaps illuminate a 'particularly mysterious moment: The Birth of Venus, which must not be confused with the birth of love. Our senses awaken before or after our hearts; never at the same time.' As he looked back over four

AN AUGUST EVENING

(COTE D'AZUR)

The future,
Here
The lady predicts it,
But not
On fête days,
When you cross the viaduct.

The maids of honours,
That goes without saying,
Allow themselves to be escorted.

What are you complaining about?
Is it my fault
If those oarsmen
go hard at it.

In the tumblers
Orangeade grows tepid.

Just any
August evening.

Littérature, 1919

published under the title *Côte d'Azur* in 1920 edition of
Les Joues en feu

years, he had seen for himself what the modern reader sees today, fifty and more years after the poems and their introduction were written: Radiguet the poet will never approach Radiguet the novelist. Nevertheless, the poems were the first proof that he had gone ahead of the avant-garde and occupied new terrain on his own. The poems are not valuable simply because they are by the author of *Le Diable au corps.* They are by Raymond Radiguet and *he* cared about them as all young people care about their poems – a great deal.

This first collection of *Les Joues en feu* earned Radiguet some enemies, but naturally the name of Rimbaud was mentioned and the young poet began to feel pleased with himself. During the autumn of 1920, however, he was more preoccupied with criticism, for Jacques Doucet's interest in *chroniques* and the existence of *Le Coq* gave him the opportunity for this kind of writing. The ideas he expressed may well have been his own from the start, but they also embodied his reaction to Cocteau's ideas. The two-way influence continued and certain concepts in Radiguet's work at this period stand out as originating with Cocteau, even if Radiguet's style was more straightforward and there has never been much danger of mistaking one man's work for the other's. The last number of *Le Coq,* in November, published a farcical parody of Rimbaud, written with Cocteau, and a short text with an arrogant title, typical of Radiguet at the time – *Advice to Great Poets.* It had originally formed part of a longer work which he obviously hoped to make into a book, but he neither completed nor revised it. The *Advice* was simple: the great poet must be *banal,* everyday, not original or, what is worse, bizarre. The lowest depths are reached in the artificial style of Edmond Rostand, or 'sub-Dadaism'. Rimbaud was sometimes bizarre, Ronsard never. Mallarmé avoided the bizarre, although he was 'too original'. Apollinaire was not sufficiently 'precious' in the best sense of the word. If true elegance should not be noticed – this recalls a famous remark by Cocteau about Beau Brummel – some 'well-born' people *do* notice it. Some composers were banal, so were three poets, Max Jacob, Jean Cocteau and 'Permit me to keep silent about the third for. . . .

'It is good to feign everything, even modesty.'

The line about himself has been identified as a quotation from one of his favourite poets, André Chénier, who had been devoted to Classical Greece and had died on the guillotine in 1794 at the age of thirty-two.

There was very little modesty about one longer piece of writing that occupied him in the early autumn of 1920. This was *Règle du jeu (Rule of the Game)*, written on forty-three pages of a school exercise-book, which remained in Cocteau's possession after Radiguet's death. The pages were phototyped with care and published in 1957, complete with all errors of spelling and grammar, notes written on the verso pages, and second thoughts. Cocteau prefaced the work in proud elegiac mood, quoting two lines by Verlaine about his young friend who had died of typhoid, and making two references to his own activities. The Rimbaud miracle, he says, and the Radiguet miracle, remain unequalled. He speaks of Radiguet's knowledge of style, his solitude. While he himself was writing *Le Secret professionnel,* 'Radiguet was seeking the rules of a new order that would overcome avant-garde fashions and illuminate the contrast between a bad scholar and a Chinese philosopher. He was both.' The *Règle du jeu* notes, he wrote, would help to clear up the 'scandal' caused by Dada activities, a rose-like bomb which 'demolished the dogmas of a period of academic anarchy'.

Cocteau did not advocate the publication of notes and drafts but he decided 'to submit to the attentive reader' some of the bouts 'in the duel fought by this Jacob against the angel of the bizarre'. Readers would find in the text that 'grimace' or wry expression with which Radiguet laughed at all other forms of grimace and the way he cocked a snook – and always would do – at 'all the vulgarities of the world'.

RULE OF THE GAME

Advice to myself

I give you the key, but without humility, as the vanquished gives it to the victor. Most writers hesitate to confide their secrets to the public, but there is no secret.

This Foreword – a far from brilliant parade, I admit, but purposely drab, in order to attract fewer people to the show inside.[1]

And those who could have been interested by The Preconceived Notion of Success will be able to read the more personal notes that follow this essay, which I have called: Advice to Great Poets. It is a favour which nobody will abuse, for people do ask to go backstage. They sometimes ask to go backstage at the theatre for reasons that are hardly austere, but it's not the same at the circus. I know of nothing more austere or chaste than the dressing-room of a clown.

End of September 1920

The Preconceived Notion of Success

We can try in vain, attempts at ill-treating geniuses never succeed. Nothing can harm them. But if it were in any way possible to ill-treat them Verlaine seems to have played a nasty trick when he christened Rimbaud, Mallarmé and himself *poètes maudits* [accursed poets].[2] In fact he admits it himself since he begins his book with this sentence: 'In order to keep calm one should say *poètes absolus,* absolute poets.'

This preconceived notion of *poésie maudite,* and consequently of success, which starts with Baudelaire* and ends today, is the thing that will have done us most harm, although it was necessary.

It may be naïve to think that all successful authors have talent, but it is even more naïve to think that an author of talent *cannot* be successful. And the most absurd thing of all is to think that an author has talent because he is not successful. And yet, in short, that is what has been happening for the last fifty years. The various generations of the last sixty years, particularly that of the symbolists, think more or less that way. We have seen miserable poets like Saint-Pol Roux or P. N. Roinard elevated to the rank of great poets simply because they did not occupy the place they deserve (a very minor place, obviously, but, after all, the one granted to them by the readers of *Les Annales* is even

* It starts earlier, but in a book which is consciously written in large letters like this one, we have to be precise.

more minor).[3] All this is the result of *'not keeping calm'*. But we shall not blame young people for that, since nothing is more detestable than young people without passionate feelings.

I prefer those who even have a passion for what is bad (the admirers of Paul-Napoléon Roinard for example).

An art form triumphs when it has talent on its side. Reason for the obscurity of the revolutionary pre-war poets: little talent — and a lot of talent in les annales *now it's the contrary*

But we must really tell ourselves that the most successful writers are those who have the most talent *in their own field.* Some academic poets are full of talent, others have none, just as within so-called *poésie maudite* there are good and bad poets. The mistake lies in preferring bad *poètes maudits* to good academic poets. It goes without saying that of all these poets the bad academic poet is the most detestable, since the academic genre rests only on immediate success. Now an unsuccessful academic poet is unforgivable in the same way as a dishonest man who has missed his chance and derives no profit from it.

But in the field of so-called popular poetry, which we cannot really approve of, we are forced to recognize that François Coppée[4] is full of talent. And I feel for him the liking, or at least the admiration, that one feels for a dishonest man whose dishonesty is not only suspected by no one but forms the source of all his honours.

Note. Alphonse Daudet and O. Feuillet.

When the young people to whom I refer look at a successful author, they no longer see the author; they see only success. And success seems to them a hateful thing, they hate this author, without being able to find justification for this hatred in his work. This is what has happened to many novelists, including some great ones like Alexandre Dumas, and others like Octave

Feuillet who are just excellent novelists. And the same is true of dramatists, like Labiche, for even at the risk of being accused of bad taste, I have no hesitation in putting him well above the place allotted to him by even the most indulgent minds. Isn't *An Italian Straw Hat* one of our favourite plays; isn't it, Max Jacob, and you Jean Cocteau? There is the true *'maudit'*, poor Labiche, who has been anathematized by the *beaux esprits*!

The entire public is bored (or, what is worse, they laugh) when they see the excellent melodramas which are performed during the summer, from August onwards. And Labiche doesn't even amuse provincials any more. Last year I saw the audience at the Odéon grousing at the performance of *An Italian Straw Hat*. I confess I found it madly entertaining; and (at the risk of being condemned myself by the *beaux esprits*, if that hasn't happened already) I confess I find it hard to understand what makes people respect Molière's coarsest farces and yet pour scorn on Labiche's plays. The public has been put on an insipid diet and likes to smile; it no longer enjoys laughing. Molière makes you laugh. Labiche makes you laugh. Audiences have been taught to respect Molière, but not yet to respect Labiche. The latter's plays bore them, but *they dare not be bored* by those of Molière. For I think audiences are sincere, just as all artists are sincere. But these two groups must contain people whose sincerity resides precisely in lying: à propos the former group it is possible to turn my sentence round the other way and say *that they dare not* laugh at Labiche's plays. It comes to the same thing in both cases, since they don't laugh. They're not

Not a day passes without people asking us if Satie or Picasso are sincere. No one ever wonders if the public is sincere in its hates and loves.

bored, purely out of decency. And this is where one must know if audiences are sincere, for in almost everyone politeness takes the place of sincerity.

I can already see a certain reader following me too quickly down this over-gentle slope that I'm offering him – in reality steeper than a hill – for the problem here consists in not letting oneself roll down to the bottom, in spite of all the pleasure that might produce. I can see this reader getting me wrong: 'How right you are! And to think there are people who don't like either Eugène Labiche or Emile Augier.'

Dear Sir, whose approval is based on misapprehension, you must know that Labiche is very good but Emile Augier is very bad.[5]

I can see also another, more perceptive reader, who may not admire my performance but at least finds it ingenious and a good way of passing a wet afternoon; he questions me: 'Among the authors who are successful, and consequently to be despised, you quote a great novelist, Alexandre Dumas, a great dramatist, Eugène Labiche, but you don't give us the name of a great poet.'

This is because poetry is such a secret thing that I think it is really difficult, almost impossible, for a poet to be truly great without being just a little secret. What is possible for the novel and the theatre is not possible for poetry. And this is why Verlaine was right when he applied the epithet *maudit* to absolute poets. But he was right in a hyperbolic way, his lack of calm leading him to hyperbole. And all the trouble was due to the fact that something which had only a poetic reality was assumed to have the reality of platitude.

And no absolute poet, any more than an absolute novelist or playwright, will have what are called big successes. Those that he will enjoy may be less sensational but they will be of better quality. This is the kind of success enjoyed by Rimbaud and Stendhal. For when I mention Alexandre Dumas you must realize that I place Stendhal above him. – But the novel and the theatre do not require the same secrecy as poetry and I could enjoy the work of a Dumas or a Labiche without liking the poets who as far as success is concerned are their equals: François Coppée, for example. And to choose an example even more illustrious than all the others, Victor Hugo.

The case of Victor Hugo is infinitely more complicated. It must be said, before we reach a conclusion, that events always served his fame. He always brought politics into things and by so doing he escapes us. But without any doubt his fame would have been hardly less resounding. For Victor Hugo, a remarkable inventor and above all a *clever man* (Baudelaire was able to see this at a time when the only word that could suitably be mentioned à propos Victor Hugo was *genius*) is first and foremost a popularizer: each of his books popularizes a form of art, a whole epoch, or simply a writer. He takes hold of everything, popularizes everything, even his own death.

History, a period of art, and sometimes even a writer, as in *Les Châtiments,* where he is not unaware of Agrippa d'Aubigné, or in *Chansons des rues et des bois,* the precious poets, and especially Tristan L'Hermite. He does not plagiarize, he popularizes. And let us not forget that he popularizes himself, for Victor Hugo

He makes use of everything, nothing does him any harm.

has nonetheless introduced a novelty into our literature. It is difficult, we must admit, to be intoxicated by the perfume of this novelty, for he immediately waters down any essence, new or old. He makes *Victor Hugo* out of everything, medieval poems, seventeenth-century poems and even his own poems! Victor Hugo, that clever man, was lucky enough to be an enthusiast; his enthusiasm saves everything; this enthusiasm is what he owes to his genius and it places him a thousand times higher than all the popularizers, although he remains more than their king, almost their god. – And it is for this reason that the general public, who value popularizers more than anyone else, admire him. Truth sometimes emerges from the mouths of fools. Once, in a train, I heard one of the latter say that if one had the complete works of Victor Hugo one could do without any other book. He was not wrong, since Hugo popularizes everything: not only our literature, our art, our folklore, but also that of every country. I agree with that stupid man, but I must admit that I prefer to read all the books in the original rather than in Hugo's translation.

It is also a good reason why those of us who prefer the original texts do not read him.

But he made the mistake of adding: 'Victor Hugo is the Bible of Modern Times.' For the reverse is the case. Since the Bible contains in embryo all that the Victor Hugos and sub-Victor Hugos were to popularize throughout the centuries. For the Bible is also much less a résumé of all vanished civilizations than a prophecy: the Bible is more concerned with the future than the past. No book is more obscure, more mysterious than the Bible. And if I had to choose a book as the Bible for Modern Times (I see absolutely no point in it, but this stupid man's remark forces me to do so), I will [*sic*] choose the work of Rimbaud.

In fact I am not displeased by this opportunity which is offered to me to assert my admiration for Rimbaud, for it will allow me to criticize him more freely throughout this book, and without any fear of being taken for one of his enemies.

François Coppée is one of those who, after an honourable start, gave in to what Jean Cocteau calls 'the peace propositions from the public'. From that day he was lost. His case is not unique and other examples can be seen, even more frequently than among writers, in numerous academic painters such as [*Boldini, crossed out*] Carolus-Duran, whose early pictures are his best.[6]

When one risks the statement that a great poet cannot have huge successes the reply is always the same: 'And what about the romantics? Weren't they successful?' For someone unaccustomed to reflection this reply can appear disturbing for half a second. But we have just examined the case of Hugo. Let us go on to Lamartine, who, in fact, was content to popularize himself. As for Musset, who was the greatest poet, or at least the most pleasant to read, his case is slightly different. With Musset, who is now despised (because of his 'sentimental' side, so decried today, but since the subject has only a secondary importance for us, we are not much concerned with the subjects he chose), with Musset, as with Verlaine later, it was not the *quality* which touched the public but what he talked about, which for the public always constitutes poetry: love, moonlight. As for Verlaine, who will soon be just as universally despised by the young as Musset, he would be already if he had not taken care to include himself among the ranks of the *poètes maudits.* And once more it is this preconceived notion of

Cf. In Francois Coppee's Le Reliquaire *it is possible to discern a certain new type of banality, although it is contained in a poem by G. de Nerval:* La Cousine, *see in* La Boheme galante.

success, which is persistent, that saved him.

There would be no point in belittling the great fascination that romance exerts over everyone. We needn't blush at it. Yet it is a somewhat undemanding fascination, when you think that the mere mention of a dove is enough to create poetry. Nevertheless, you can create poetry by mentioning a dove, but first of all you must forget everything that your predecessors have said about it.

But fortunately the poets without personality are those who have the best memory. It is just as easy for the others to be creative if they are talking about a dove or a shirt-collar. Apollinaire did not know how to do this, although his scope was wide. But he takes things too much as they are; he says 'my dove' to his beloved, instead of seeing the dove as an everyday object, and he speaks of his shirt-collar as an everyday object, without trying to make it poetic! In both cases he creates nothing. (Naturally I am pointing out what constitutes the weakness of Apollinaire's work, but I can just as easily state what gives it its strength. Unfortunately this is not the place for that.)

The classic works without worrying about anything: if about something, it's about pleasing. But certainly not displeasing.

As for Vigny, don't talk to me about his success. It is small. Of all the romantics Vigny is the only one who makes no concessions to the public. In that, he is more classic than romantic. For the classic seeks neither applause nor boos. The romantic is avid for both. He is ready to make every concession in order to win the favour of being booed or applauded. And if that were all I needed in order to prove that a recent school christened *Dada* is romantic, it would be enough for me. Not that Dada wants to be applauded. On the contrary, Dada is ready to make every concession, provided it gets boos from the public. And that is why Dada organizes uproars worthy of schoolboys, art student jokes. How close the students from the Ecoles des Beaux-Arts are to you, my poor Dadaists.

Yet one whole side of Vigny is romantic, for the *poète maudit,* a romantic prejudice, naturally, was invented by Vigny, and it is in Chatterton that the expression, taken up by Baudelaire and Verlaine, finds all its strength. The preface to Vigny's masterpiece.

Success

Let us take for example the theatre, for if a book can live without knowing success, the same is not true of the theatre, at first glance.

However, there as elsewhere, true success is not what one thinks it is. How many plays performed at the boulevard theatres achieve three hundred performances. However, two months after the last performance nobody remembers the title of the play. On the other hand absolutely everyone talked about and are still talking about the ballet that was performed five times in Paris, *Parade*, which provoked what I would call a *scandale* of classic proportions; *Parade* was not devised for the purpose of being booed, unlike *Les Mamelles de Tirésias,* a rather tedious farce, in which Apollinaire was much less concerned with reviving the theatre than with provoking a *scandale.*[7] As happens in cases like this, and as happened to the Dadaists later, Apollinaire was truly punished: his play made nobody angry. One critic, who was perceptive for once, wrote that *Les Mamelles de Tirésias* could have been signed by Henri Lave-

It was seen as a highly moral little comedy.

dan. This was certainly not what Apollinaire had wanted. Except when it is a question of explaining, as in this book, a writer must never think about the audience. Apollinaire made the mistake of thinking about the audience, in a different way no doubt from the writers for the boulevard theatre, but he did think about them.

Finally, let it be clearly said, no fame is more dazzling than the fame of the *poètes maudits*: (Of the six *poètes maudits* studied by Verlaine, I am thinking only of Rimbaud, Mallarmé, then of Verlaine and finally of Desbordes-Valmore and of *Pauvre Lélian* himself). I insist on believing that Villiers de l'Isle-Adam and Tristan Corbière have been included by mistake among the absolute poets. Villiers de l'Isle-Adam, whose personality was more astonishing to his contemporaries than his work (it is now old-fashioned) like the title of one of his books: *Contes cruels,* and Corbière, who only astonished his age and only astonishes now because we are used to seeing Breton bards applauded and he is a bard who is booed.[8]

both of them slightly sentimental because both very feminine natures. Verlaine bearded lady.

But no fame, not even Hugo's, is more overwhelming than that of Rimbaud. Only one must know how to distinguish between genuine and false success. The romantics confused everything: they were the first to experience big editions. It is too often thought that Stendhal did not know what success was; he was simply introducing a new form of success, which later on was going to be that of Rimbaud, Mallarmé and others. In one year eight copies of a book by Beyle were sold, but that did not prevent Sainte-Beuve from writing of him: 'Stendhal, simultaneously trumpet-major and vanguard general of the new literary revolution.' And as soon as his works were sold out their prices rose to incredible heights for the period. But for his colleagues, *nouveaux riches* of literature, such a success must have seemed a failure.

A writer should be proud of his work. He is naturally pleased by the admiration shown to him. But he has less reason to be proud of his influence, inevitably bad, whatever his work is like. One is right only for oneself and from a relative point of view.

When I say that the public values popularizers, it should not be thought that by public I mean only the general public. Everyone likes popularizers. And the proof is that everyone believes this absurd legend about *precursors.* As though there were any precursors! When people talk to me about precursors I cannot prevent myself from thinking of a ridiculous gentleman who goes out with an umbrella on a fine day, a mathematician who makes a calculation of improbabilities. How can there be precursors, since imitators don't count. Does Rimbaud only exist because he has imitators? His influence, and that of Mallarmé, do not interest me at all. It is their work that I enjoy, that is all, and not in any way the harm that they might have done within the brains of young people. This is why the comparative method, dear to critics, is of no use to me, for each poet should be examined as unique: a case that will never occur again. After that the critic will be able to amuse himself searching out what links this poet to all his predecessors but he will only do it without risk if he is convinced that a masterpiece proves nothing.

V.H. touches everything, he vulgarizes everything.

The superiority of poetry and religion over science is that science, which also feeds only on *religion — dead today — and ever since Jesus — since there are no more miracles.*

miracles, wants to admit only those miracles which do not repeat themselves. The scientist therefore is concerned with tracking them down, harnessing them, taming them and in this way even weakening them. It is a mistake therefore to say that the scientist is a poet after his fashion. Rather, the scientist is a critic; he wishes to profit from the lesson of the past. Now, one doesn't profit from the lesson of the past. and if by chance there were some scientist who was content to be a poet, the censure that his colleagues would inflict on him would soon bring him back into line. How at this juncture could one fail to remember Henri Poincaré's splendid sentence which Jean Cocteau quotes in *Le Potomak.* 'Every day brings us a new miracle in our laboratories, but responsibility obliges us to maintain a professional silence; the faith people have in us can only be maintained by certainty.'

It is not for me to decide which of the two, poet or critic, is more important than the other. To anyone who believes in progress, criticism has a more certain value than poetry! But poetry, precisely because it is not trying to prove the miracle or link it to this or that system, is richer in its teaching. The respect of a scientist like Henri Poincaré for poetry (respect with which is mingled regret for his incapacity to create poetry) is conclusive.

And critics in their scepticism would like to assimilate poetry with science since at each miracle (that is: at each new work), they say: and now we are waiting for an opus.

We do not draw any profit from the famous *lesson of the past*: how fortunate! It would be pointless to think that we are taking a step forward. We never take a step forward. Let us say rather that each step we take is taken in another direction. And don't let anyone speak to us about a swan song, or say: 'Everything has been said. We arrive too late in a world that is too old.' I think, on the contrary, that if many things have been said, there remain even more to say. Just as there are always young men in the world, in the same way the earth is no older than during the first days after its birth.

Half past 4 in the afternoon.

Thursday 7 October – 9 o'clock in the morning.

Let nobody say: if the public applauds without rhyme or reason it is the artists' fault for they do not think about educating the public. One cannot educate them; the public is incapable of improvement, and this is one more proof that the world has not grown older. Once writers who were unsuccessful in their time are dead, the public is taught to respect them: the public cannot be educated, for that is impossible, *they are taught a lesson,* they are given a *veneer* of culture, but they always go back to their first loves, which repeat themselves in a new form.

The question of the public's sincerity is more serious than one thinks. In my opinion only the applause or the boos which greet a new play (to take as an example the theatre, the only field of observation for the *immediate*) can be sincere. They do not come to order. They are reflexes. But in this it is important not to see in a theatre auditorium an assembly of 1,000 or 2,000 people, each one possessing an individuality. For, on entering, each spectator takes off his individuality in the cloakroom, together with his overcoat. This is what is so well expressed in the admirable phrase: 'Evening dress obligatory', indicating that one is no longer a man different from the rest, but a sheep going back into the flock, avoiding in this way metaphors from military language, to which literary slang already owes so much (avant-garde writers etc.). An audience is either bored or entertained. The objection will be made, to take a famous example once again, that *Parade* had violent detractors and supporters. But that does not destroy this argument in any way. In the same way, whenever we do something part of our personality rebels and the other part submits. In the case I am talking about, the phenomenon is apparent instead of being concealed, taking place within.

It is always good form to speak ill of snobs. If one admits that sheep have a right to live, do not speak ill of snobs, who are more intelligent sheep, or at least led by more intelligent shepherds.

Not only does an audience possess individuality, but like a man it becomes accustomed to it. Do not think that at each performance, with different spectators, the same thing begins again. One might be tempted to believe it: for the novelty, still unknown to these spectators, is less of a *shock* to those who attend the second performance than to those who attend the first. And so on. For if the play is really alive, the first performance has always a slightly primitive quality, like a birth. Then, to other performances, come the parents, the friends. The baby is at last firmly settled in his cradle and nobody thinks any longer of refusing him the right to live. Gradually people become too accustomed to the play. In this individuality of an audience there is a phenomenon much more important (although of the same order) than that of table-turning.

Novelty is like those too-new plays which the public, suspicious, rejects, because they have never seen them before.

The public, which sees no further than the end of its nose, accepts every day phoney plays reproducing exactly those to which it is accustomed. As for new plays, the public accuses them of being counterfeit, as if forgers amused themselves making coins which had never been seen before! It is only when the new play has become worn (and as a result liable to be imitated, because it is already known) that the public will consider it to be 'legal tender'.

Scientists are popularizers. The great scientist, like the man who is called a great poet, will be the man who like Hugo popularizes the miracles of other people and his own. It can be regretted that in the realm of science there is no absolute poet. Of course if he existed he would have to expect to be treated as good, genius does not prove itself.

The public are suspicious. They always believe that people are laughing at them.

The public are suspicious about artists: artists are not suspicious enough about the public.

People speak of the injustice of the present and of justice within time, within eternity. The eternal legend of the author who is booed during his lifetime, while after his death his works are taught in schools.

This is true, but it should not be seen as a proof of clairvoyance on the part of the public, a tardy clairvoyance, but clairvoyance all the same: those who lead the public have time to become aware, to accept the evidence. Teachers of literature, who are slightly more clairvoyant than the public, are forced to recognize that Racine is superior to Pradon.[9] And it is because schoolchildren are taught to like Racine that they do like him. Suppose for a moment that teachers perpetuated the mistake made by the public, and Pradon were taught in schools, children would find that splendid too and would grumble just as much about having to learn his lines as about learning those of Racine.

In the first place this is not true, for I doubt whether the absolute poets, Rimbaud, Mallarme, will ever be taught in schools; but I shall not consider myself accursed if my poems are not taught in schools.

The public's unfairness is sincere, it does not

come to order. Its so-called fairness is instilled into it from birth. But as soon as it is left to itself, to its own free will, that is when a living author is fed to it, someone about whom nothing conclusive has been said, then the public applauds Coppée and sniggers at Rimbaud!

So let nobody talk about progress.

Write legibly.

Do the readers of *Les Annales,* to whom this paper offers each week several so-called 'comprehensible' poems, suspect that these poems (so clear!) mean nothing to their authors. (If I don't say: 'are meaningless to their authors', this is because the word 'meaningless' has been weakened.) And by 'mean nothing' I mean that these poems possess no deep meaning.

The enemies of Rimbaud and Mallarmé have not failed to say that these two authors were incomprehensible, unreadable, finally that they wrote just anything. No, if there are authors who write just anything (which is not in fact the same thing as: anything, since an author who decides to write just anything would never write everything that went through his head) they are really the poets dear to the readers of *Les Annales.* There are others: a few of our most advanced Dadaists. (And if their poems are so different and even seem at the opposite extreme [apparently] from the poets of *Les Annales,* it is because everything that goes through the heads of our Dadaists is different – most fortunately – from the thoughts of the academic poets.) But here and there, the same method of working ('the absence of system is also a system, but the most attractive of them all,' writes Tristan Tzara, who, through his very scope, is above Dadaism, in the same way as Mallarmé is not Mallarmian). And Dadaist poets seem to me hardly more interesting than academic poets. Moreover I will establish a parallel between them at more length.

Admirers of Rimbaud and Mallarmé were bound to recognize that in fact these authors are obscure, and to seek out reasons for their obscurity, each one having his own, very different, and for reasons which are also very different; but neither of them being as difficult as a puzzle. Mallarmé's obscurity existed for him. Rimbaud's exists only for his readers. Rimbaud is certainly the author who was less concerned than anyone else in the world about writing for anything except his own personal pleasure. Since concern for the reader does not enter into his work for a single moment there can be no question for him of obscurity or clarity. He always remains intelligible for himself, as clear as crystal, and if his clarity is not that of his reader the latter is forced to discover this, all the same. The advantage of an obscure work, like *Les Illuminations,* is that even the most intelligent mind discovers on reading it for the thousandth time a new and intimate meaning which had not appeared to him earlier.

Mallarmé's obscurity does not come from the same source. Mallarmé, if he cared little about his contemporary public, cared infinitely about his future readers, he thinks only of them and in order that his thought could reach them intact, he disguises it and surrounds it with obscurity. This is what gives his work, which is not very alive, the grace of a mummy. I am speak-

The lifelessness of his work is due to the fact that it clings too much to life.

ing here of the obscurity of his poems in verse, which I rate much higher than the poem JAMAIS UN COUP DE DES N'ABOLIRA LE HASARD, which is all the same so mysterious and fascinating, and especially of his prose: DIVAGATIONS, which is his most inferior work. If the reasons for this obscurity are not less noble than those for the obscurity of his verses, the achievement is certainly less so. True courage does not consist of letting oneself be killed for nothing; on the contrary, the hero is the man who clings to life. The beauty of Mallarmé's verses lies in the fact that they do not wish to die. On the contrary, Mallarmé's prose, like a useless heroine, dedicates itself to certain death. In DIVAGATIONS S. Mallarmé has had the courage – fatal – not to write as people speak. The result is that one cannot read aloud a single page of his prose without being horribly shocked. In his prose Mallarmé avoids *le mot juste* like the plague, preferring instead the rare word, the periphrasis of those *précieuses ridicules* whose language Molière reports to us, without exaggerating it.

This proves to us that one cannot, even if one wanted to, do without the commonplace which must not be confused with the cliche of which it is the opposite. Depending on whether it is handled by a popular author or not, the commonplace is popular or precious. If it is popular it lacks strength; it is the task of the talented writer to make it precious. By doing without the commonplace poetry risks becoming artificial. And nothing is more common than artificiality. Lalique jewellery, all art nouveau, is a striking example of it. Don't confuse 'artificial' with 'precious.' Gold is precious, poetry is precious.

But if the language of the *précieuses* was sometimes incomprehensible, their vocabulary did not contain the lifeless words used by Mallarmé and which make you want to read his prose with the accent of a policeman.[10] In fact, these DIVAGATIONS are like police reports. In reality, Mallarmé is only pursuing the method used by all writers and taking it, with an unshakeable logic, beyond the limits of the possible; no one decides to write like everyone else, believing that to do so would be to sacrifice his originality, while in fact the discipline that every writer with a personality should inflict on himself is the search for the commonplace.

Don't confuse artifice and artificial convention, all characters in novels or plays are conventional but bad if artificial

Treatises on the art of writing (and I know one of them, without any author's name, as is fitting, and one which is never far away from me) possess the excellent quality of telling you, more or less: Write legibly. This is also what parents say to their children, when they have to send best wishes for the New Year; children like adults being only too inclined to imagine that their ideal handwriting is like a doctor's, unreadable. (Parents will never suspect the excellence of the principles they inculcate into their children. One excellent remark out of a thousand, from family training: don't keep looking round – In the street – And when their child reaches the age of twenty the parents object because the child does not keep his eyes continually fixed on the past!) Just as parents do not know *why* the upbringing they give to their children is good, professors of literature, and those of an institution like the Ecole des Beaux-Arts, do not guess at the reasons why we respect them.

(1) Vocabulary note — about the word precious — banal — original.

scrawly handwriting, glamour of black books.

It is in the order of things that a writer seeks what he has not got. Let a mediocre writer try to be original, let an original writer try to be ordinary. It is because he spurned oddness too much that someone like Rimbaud often spoils his masterpieces for us through this quality. Mallarmé, who is rarely odd, does not, in the admirable part of his work (his verse), seek out originality, metaphor; he never explores. It is precisely this contained strength (we can see an example of it in the drawings of Picasso where the line   )

Here a sentence about Picasso's drawings.

that gives birth to beauty.

It is natural for Edmond Rostand[11] to seek out originality; it is less so for Mallarmé, who only needs to be slightly banal. I admit it took me a long time to understand (and others will probably be like me) why Mallarmé was Edmond Rostand's favourite poet, since on Edmond Rostand's part this is equivalent to the admission that he has not done what he wanted to do. But one is blind as far as oneself is concerned and on examining the work I can see resemblances, distant ones, but they can exist. Mallarmé, always on the verge of bad taste, never falls over the precipice. Rostand who is always Rostand, weakened by this constant search for originality and artificiality, must have admired in Mallarmé the conduct of which he was incapable. Both of them have read the 'precious' poets; but I doubt whether they read the same ones. Rostand knows them especially through the intervention of the Hugo of the *Chansons des rues et des bois.* But among all these 'precious' poets Tristan L'Hermite[12] is a great one, it is to him that Rostand owes most. But Mallarmé's prose (all *quality* apart), but [*sic*] as exhausting as Edmond Rostand's poetry, supplies us with the clue to this enigma. For it is certain that only the bad parts of Mallarmé can appeal to a Rostand.

It has often occurred to me while writing to compare Rostand's poetry with Dadaist poetry. I shall explain myself without further delay. Rostand thinks only of applause. Any self-respecting Dadaist thinks only of boos. First point of resemblance: preoccupation with the public. This preoccupation leads them to neglect art, and both of them to write poems without mean-

Here is what L(ouis) A(ragon), *with whom I exchanged poems, wrote to me a year and a half ago, he was still in the army, already ripe for Dadaism: 'I want to reproach you.*

ing. An effort at originality, from both of them; and the same originality, obtained by different methods.

Your two poems had delighted me at first, I showed them to other people, they liked them. That really spoils them for me, I assure you. You aren't the least bit shocking.'

So it's been said, that big word! le scandale. *You must be shocking, giving pleasure is a mortal sin. Now if one must choose absolutely, I prefer to please rather than displease.*

That's their game: they must displease! Mine is pleasing without cheating.

5 o'clock in the afternoon.

10 o'clock in the morning – Friday.

Prodigies

'These prodigies, prematurely intelligent, who a few years later become prodigies of stupidity.' What family does not possess its child prodigy? They have made a mockery of the word. There are child prodigies just as there are adult prodigies. They are rarely the same. Age is nothing. The child prodigy is too often a monster. One is never advanced for one's age. It is not the age at which Rimbaud wrote that surprises me. It is his work. It is a mistake to believe that it is rare to see adolescents of sixteen writing. There are only too many of them. A Russian friend said to me: But in fact there have been few poets of seventeen. I corrected him: Nothing is less rare than poets of seventeen. Young men of talent are more rare. But men are almost as rare. All great poets have written at seventeen. But the greatest are those who have succeeded in making us forget it. Hugo wrote at seventeen, but the works of his eightieth year make us forget it. Rimbaud wrote at fifteen: the works of his nineteenth year make me forget it. *Les Illuminations,* much better than the first poems by him that we know. And nothing prevents us from supposing that, if he had continued to

I am choosy about words.

Rimbaud didn't want to make people forget them. One can see therefore

write (we must not think that he wrote no more because his genius had dried up), the works of his thirtieth year would have been far superior to *Les Illuminations.*

On the contrary if I wrote no more this could be through weakness, through fear of not being able to make people forget my first work.

You only go on writing in order to forget yourself and make others forget what you have just writen.

The last born is always the most beautiful, afterwards you make judgements.

You write in order to earn forgiveness for the works you wrote before.

Always reject oneself.

One publishes to get rid of something.

Let us not blame Rousseau for entrusting his children to the foundling hospital.
That is what we are doing.

When a poet makes his début as a child, if he is great (and enduring), his mature poems will cause his childhood poems to be forgotten, although this does not mean they are bad. Genius consists in making unreadable, works written at seventeen which the greatest poets of the time describe as remarkable. That is what genius should do.

To a recent enquiry: Why do you write? Monsieur Valéry replied: From weakness. I believe on the contrary that the weakness would be not writing. Rimbaud stopped writing, doubting himself, and in order to preserve his memory. Through fear of not being able to do better. (Those timid people who daren't show their work because they are waiting for it to improve should not see this as an excuse for their weakness. For if one is interesting one's first efforts will be interesting too.) In a certain sense one never does better, one never does worse.

Monday – 9 o'clock in the morning.

The fable, which did not exist before La Fontaine (for Phaedrus and Aesop wrote only for La Fontaine), cannot exist after him. Florian(!).[13] For the fable, a tedious genre if ever there was one; La Fontaine's genius consists in this: after him one cannot imagine any other fables except his. Moreover, since his imitators don't count, full stop new paragraph. The only thing to do is to abandon him. This is why we can see in his Fables the typical masterpiece.

and its definition

It is not a question of knowing if the fable, conceived in some other way, could have produced more. The word fable being inseparable from the name of La Fontaine.

to shock less for Hugo to state truths in a less hurtful way.

In the same way today, I cannot see the phrase 'prose poem' without feeling uneasy, unless Max Jacob is then mentioned; these two names are inseparable. Obviously others before him attempted this genre; it is not a question of knowing whether, in another range of ideas, Fables composed before or after La Fontaine [*sic*]. Just as saying of La Fontaine that he is the creator of the fable is false, since there were fables in all ages, in the same way it is false and yet true that Max Jacob 'created the prose poem'. Before him one thinks of something suspect, neither verse nor prose, musical prose. Max Jacob's prose poems are written in a familiar language, in an everyday style, as everything should be written! And the author of *Le Cornet à dés* failed only in not having been a little more severe in the selection of his poems. Max Jacob has manuscripts in his house, about three volumes of prose poems. He should publish them. And later I can imagine fairly easily a selection of his prose poems.

It is a commonplace to say that the century of Louis XIV is a century of plagiarists reconcile that with

Apollinaire, Max Jacob told me, did not accept being matter-of-fact.

These words have been used in a narrow rather than in a broad sense but all the better

Max Jacob and La Fontaine have not invented genres. La Fontaine does not set the rules of the fable.

And, on seeing the scorn of some poets for Max Jacob's admirable work, I can easily imagine the reasons why in his *art poétique* Boileau omits the fable from his nomenclature of genres. For him the word has another meaning: La Fontaine was not sufficiently serious, like Max Jacob today. And his fables only encountered a certain success during his lifetime thanks to the extreme modesty of the title: Fable by Aesop put into verse by Monsieur de La Fontaine! For us it is no longer a question of knowing whether there were fable-writers before La Fontaine. The fable did not exist before him, it cannot exist after him. It can be said that this genre is dead. The same is true of the prose poem: Max Jacob has killed it in taking it to the same degree of perfection, in making it HIS thing, as La Fontaine did for the fable. André Breton seems to commit a grave error in reproaching Max Jacob for having made the prose poem into a game with rules one can learn, as with the sonnet. I know that a sonnet consists of two quatrains and two tercets. I would like you to tell me, my dear Breton, the exact length of a prose poem. The sonnet is not a genre, it is a poem of fixed form. Thanks to Max Jacob the prose poem has become a genre, in the same way as the fable, the idyll and the eclogue, which obey rules but not those of versification.[14]

poem in a regular form

* * *

The MS. breaks off here and no further notes exist about how Radiguet intended to continue. After his experience in writing reviews for Jacques Doucet and the magazine *Le Coq,* Radiguet now felt sure of himself and of his abilities as a writer and critic. With Olympian arrogance he felt ready to tackle the whole of French literature and the insoluble problems of how to please a theatre audience. He wanted to tell everyone, not merely his friends, that he advocated a kind of commonsense anti-modernism that selected what was lasting in the 'old' values and presented this choice in a new way, new because he was young enough to have an uncluttered mind and cared little about what people said. He did, however, care a great deal about what *he* said, and never took himself more seriously than he does in *Règle du jeu.* The piece shows how fast he was developing and how his prose style was moving ahead of the Cocteau-like epigrams of the early articles to plain interpretative statements. When he came to write novels it was this aspect of his style that impressed most, and still does – the directness and the analytic flashes which avoid platitude and express truths in a way which does not date.

Down with Victor Hugo, he was a mere popularizer; down with Dada, it is more tedious than the so-called academicism that it attacks. Down with Mallarmé as a prose writer and three cheers for Labiche for he can make us laugh. 'Us' in the text specifically includes Max Jacob and Jean Cocteau, as though Radiguet were still asking for support from his well-known elders and at the same time thanking them for their help. The references at the beginning to the circus parade and the chaste austerity of clown's dressing-rooms show that Cocteau was not far away. The two men were still working together on not very serious writing for the theatre and Cocteau was certainly at least planning his well-known essay *Le Secret professionnel.* This very phrase occurs in *Règle du jeu* and one wonders who in fact used it first, for there are many points of contact between the two texts. As for the remarks about prodigies, Radiguet was obviously keen to dismiss them and – more important – not to be regarded as one himself.

Radiguet's work on *Règle du jeu* may have been interrupted by a rapid trip at the end of September to join Cocteau at Le Picquey on the bassin d'Arcachon in the Gironde. Cocteau and his friends had stayed there before and his favourite inn, Le Chantecler, was already known as an *auberge littéraire*; writers of all kinds stayed at the inn and Pierre Benoist wrote one of his novels there. On this occasion Cocteau, who had travelled alone, was trying hard to work in spite of a bad cold and expected regular letters from Radiguet because they were working together on two projects. One of them was the libretto for an *opéra-comique,* conceived earlier that year when the two of them were sitting in La Rotonde, the Montparnasse café, with the composer Erik Satie. They had talked about writing something which he could set to music. Satie had already composed the music for *Parade,* Cocteau's *ballet réaliste* of 1917 and Cocteau had praised him highly in his pamphlet *Le Coq et l'arlequin.* Radiguet suggested the theme of Bernardin de Saint-Pierre's famous novel *Paul et Virginie,* published in 1787, a tale of naïve young lovers in an exotic setting, based on the life Saint-Pierre, an admirer of Rousseau, had seen in Mauritius. Apart from his love of the classics, Radiguet had probably been influenced by the fact that his mother came from a Creole family and had been born in Martinique. So he felt doubly involved.

However, the story had to be adapted, for the Cocteau circle would have found the 'innocence' of Bernardin de Saint-Pierre's characters too absurd and far from theatrical. Radiguet and Cocteau between them turned the story partly into a social satire and partly into an extraordinarily prophetic 'game of death and life'. Attempts to marry Virginie to a pompous general in Paris are used as a means of attacking the false values of the *bourgeoisie,* and the relevant act of the opera, set in the capital, is entitled 'Among the savages'. After Virginie is drowned on her way back to her exotic island she 'appears' to Paul and says she may be dead but this means she can never die, and they will 'live' happily ever after in the place they like best. Act III is called 'The true Paradise'.

Radiguet had already written a poem entitled *Paul et Virginie* and it was agreed he would compose the lyrics, sending them to Cocteau as he wrote them. The *opéra-comique Paul et Virginie* was announced in *Le Coq* and Satie's name was added to the libretto, but in fact he composed nothing and the text itself waited over forty years for publication, appearing for the first time in Italy in 1967. Some extracts had appeared in the Club des Libraires edition of the Radiguet complete works, but that was all. Not surprisingly, in fact, for this is far from a masterpiece. Cocteau's dialogue is mildly amusing but the most interesting thing about it is the 'game of death and life' which seems to foreshadow the theme of Cocteau's *Orphée* in its abolition of any barrier between the two states. Radiguet's lyrics are light and rhythmic, asking for the music they never received:

Cher Paul apprends le jeu de mourir et de vivre
Que ne nous enseigne aucun livre . . .

And as though the author were still thinking of the prose piece he had written in his exercise book, this song is called *Chanson des règles du jeu.* Other lines read:

Les morts seuls sont en vie
Car ils ne meurent pas.

Virginie's letter-song is no mere lyric but a poem in its own right and has been published as such in *Les Joues en feu.* Radiguet was expected to complete more lyrics, as the text indicates. When Paul says 'What is money?', a merchant replies, 'A very good thing' and there is a note: 'here a song about money'. Cocteau does not seem to have complained too much about the lack of lyrics because he obviously adored his young friend and did not dare complain – yet – about anything he did or did not do.

Radiguet was so full of ideas that he could not bring himself to finish one project before starting another. Cocteau suffered from the same weakness but he was by now a truly professional writer and usually finished what he began. Their other joint project was a piece just as frivolous as *Paul et Virginie* but again it had a serious starting-point, one that Radiguet had already mentioned in *Règle du jeu,* his mandarin-like attitude towards Mallarmé. He was ready to admire certain aspects of Mallarmé's poetry but had taken a violent dislike to the prose *Divagations.* He had persuaded

Cocteau to take part in writing a short play in which Mallarmé and admirers of Mallarmé would be attacked, amusingly, of course. When he joined Cocteau at Le Picquey the two men had intended to work on both the opera libretto and the anti-Mallarmé piece, called *Le gendarme incompris.* Cocteau, however, was so worried about his bad cold that Radiguet was made to stay on the balcony outside Cocteau's room so that *he* would not catch the cold. Cocteau wrote to his mother that he 'dictated' to his young friend, working from ten in the morning until three in the afternoon. Radiguet had brought with him the Mallarmé texts that Cocteau needed before the work could be completed.

This holiday ended abruptly; a day or so after his arrival Radiguet was recalled to Paris by telegram. His mother was ill. He does not seem to have questioned his filial duty; he sincerely loved his parents and if Cocteau tried to persuade him to stay he did not succeed. Radiguet returned to Paris with a group of friends who had been on a brief visit to Cocteau. Radiguet's time had not been wasted, although he did not know it then: the leader of the group, Prince Firouz of Persia, 'Prince Turquoise' as Cocteau called him, was to appear again three years later as Prince Mirza in Radiguet's second novel, *Le Bal du comte d'Orgel.*

That autumn Maurice Radiguet's concern about his son's future once again became the subject of a letter of complaint to Cocteau. The latter had to admit that he did not always know where Radiguet was and in his slightly peevish anxiety *he* began to complain too, saying that the boy continually promised work but did not produce it. Cocteau did not like to admit even to himself that his young friend occasionally disappeared, that even he did not know where he was. He also worried jealously about the company he was keeping. However, Radiguet had been close to him during the rehearsals for the revival of the ballet *Parade* and even wrote a long review of it for the daily paper *Le Gaulois,* which published it on Christmas Day.

Parade, the Cocteau-Satie-Picasso collaboration, had not been a great success in 1917 and Cocteau for one had never forgiven the audience for failing to respond to this work, which he regarded as a masterpiece. When Radiguet reviewed it he naturally praised it and, to be fair, there is every chance that this revival was better than the original performance. Radiguet, however, did not limit himself to superficial observations. First of all he gives various possible reasons for its failure in 1917; for instance, the patriotic public regarded it as Dadaist, i.e. coming from Munich, but, he adds, in reality nothing could have been more French. He compares its reception with that given to Stravinsky's *Rite of Spring,* points out that its audacity was 'interior' and moves on to more general observations: Racine at first seems less daring than Rimbaud, but in fact the quality of his audacity is more refined, 'for it took *pudeur* so far that it passed unnoticed'. He then develops his own theory that he had expressed in *Règle du jeu* and talked about so much. (Cocteau claimed that he had learnt it from Radiguet – yet once at least he had told Radiguet to put it into practice himself. Who was quoting whom? There is no way of knowing.) Radiguet goes on to say that the audiences of 1917 found the 'everyday quality' of *Parade* 'aggressive', for they were ill-informed. 'In a period of extreme complication like ours, "writing like everyone"..., when everyone tries to write like no one else, is considered to be insolent.' He concludes by insisting that the ballet was indeed 'realist' and profoundly true, that it was utterly clear and accessible. Neither does he believe that it was a 'precursor' of anything, for precursors are no more important than imitators and popularizers, another view he had expressed in *Règle du jeu.* The work would in fact be imitated, but those who had created it were going on to other, different things.

NOTES

1 A partly-conscious reference to Cocteau, his devotion to the circus, and his *ballet réaliste* of 1917, *Parade.*

2 Verlaine's famous essays, *Les Poètes maudits,* were first published in 1884. The underappreciated, 'accursed' poets were Tristan Corbière, Marceline Desbordes-Valmore, Villiers de l'Isle-Adam, Mallarmé, Rimbaud and himself, described under the anagram 'Pauvre Lélian'.

3 P. N. Roinard, a now-forgotten symbolist, to whom Apollinaire dedicated at least one poem. *Les Annales politiques et littéraires* was a 'respectable' literary journal.

4 François Coppée, 1842-1908, a popular poet and playwright known as '*le poète des humbles*'.

5 Emile Augier, 1820-1889, wrote realistic plays, often satirizing the middle classes from which he came.

6 Boldini and Carolus-Duran were two fashionable portrait-painters.

7 Radiguet takes the opportunity to praise Cocteau's *Parade* and decry Apollinaire, who had accused him of plagiary.

8 The *Contes cruels,* by Villiers de l'Isle-Adam, and Tristan Corbière's poems, are by no means neglected in 1976.

9 Nicolas Pradon, an obscure seventeenth-century dramatist used by Racine's enemies as a potential rival.

10 Radiguet attacked Mallarmé's prose in *Le Gendarme incompris,* see pp. 90-92.

11 Edmond Rostand, 1868-1918, is best remembered for his verse plays *Cyrano de Bergerac, L'Aiglon* and *Chantecler.*

12 Tristan L'Hermite, the dramatist, who lived from about 1600 to 1655.

13 Florian, 1755-1794, a lesser fable-writer and novelist.

14 Jacob's prose poems are disappointing today, but Radiguet owed him a debt of gratitude. The attack on Breton implies support for Cocteau.

1921

Much of Radiguet's writing was done away from Paris. The capital was too distracting, too full of friends, admirers, bars, restaurants, theatres, fairgrounds, and he began to share Cocteau's habit of writing by the sea. Yet his so-called holidays were a break only from the exhausting social life of the city, they were no holiday from work. In the spring of 1921, a few months before his eighteenth birthday, he borrowed some money from Lucien Daudet and took himself well away from Paris to the Mediterranean coast, choosing Carqueiranne, within reach of Toulon and Le Lavandou, famous for its sheltered bays, red rocks and handsome pine trees, and recommended by his friends Jean and Valentine Hugo. He stayed at an establishment with a delightful name, the Hôtel Gilly et Jules, which sounds grander than it was, no more than a lodging house over a bistro in fact. At this season it should have been empty and peaceful, but the inhabitants included a baby, who cried all night. Yet Radiguet must have been happy in Carqueiranne, because he worked.

'I've been in the south, by the sea,' he wrote to Jacques Doucet on April 2nd, 'for about five weeks, and I've done a tremendous lot of work. – Solitude is so good for me! and Paris so bad, from the point of view of work, which is really what interests me most.' He added that he had not been alone the whole time, because the painters Juan Gris and Pierre La Fresnaye, as well as Cocteau, had been to see him. He realized that even when working hard he could not bear to be on his own for too long, and made no claim to asceticism. 'The terrible moment,' he went on, 'when you're alone, is when you lose your balance, when you no longer know what you're doing. At that moment visits from friends are very helpful.'

He was on his own long enough to write some poetry and at least one short story. When Cocteau joined him after about three weeks the work did not stop, although it may have changed course. Both men wrote a good deal, sometimes jointly, they played literary games and at a more serious level they influenced each other's writing, as Cocteau was the first to acknowledge. He valued this closeness, this interchange, and made no secret of the fact. He wanted Radiguet to himself but could not stop him from sending his poems to friends such as Valentine Hugo. Although he naturally wanted Radiguet to publish as much as possible he believed that *he* should see all the work first and that he should arrange its publication. Radiguet's name was becoming known now, not merely as another young friend of Cocteau's, but as a creative personality whom many people disliked and gossiped about in Paris. He was thought, by those who did not know him, to be parasitic, vicious, and addicted to drink and drugs. Some people also thought him 'common', but they may have been too much aware of Cocteau's wealthy bourgeois background, where nobody lacked money and some perhaps did not know how to use it. The Radiguet family, whose genealogy included famous names, only had money when they worked for it.

The gossip inevitably reached Cocteau's mother, who wrote to her son and complained about the company he was keeping. Cocteau's belief in Radiguet was unshakeable. At the end of March he replied to his mother and tried to make it clear to her that he had not been allowing the younger man to dictate to him while living at his expense. 'Radiguet was due to leave,' he wrote. 'It was I who begged him to stay. I admire him. I respect him, and nothing or *nobody* will succeed in making me change my mind, for *my* first discipline is not to commit the injustice shown every day by religious people.' Cocteau's mother was a practising Catholic and this remark was intended to hurt. He went on to point out that his belief in Radiguet was now shared by many others, and had recently been proved in a practical fashion. 'He has received from Bernard Fay, on behalf of *The Dial* [the literary magazine] – 1000 francs which allows him to extend his stay.' Bernard Fay, a young university teacher and writer with contacts in the United States, was later to play an important part in Radiguet's career.

To friends who were more sympathetic than his mother Cocteau wrote enthusiastically about Radiguet's latest work. The poems were like 'peach-down', Radiguet's room was 'a beehive, a real honey factory'. A letter Cocteau wrote to Valentine Hugo, quoted by Francis Steegmuller in his biography of Cocteau, describes clearly how the two men influenced each other and in particular how far Cocteau's infatuation with Radiguet made him impressed, perhaps over-impressed sometimes, with the younger man's work, justifying what he was to write and repeat later about Radiguet being his 'teacher': 'My enormous poem encourages Bébé to write longer ones, and his verse is helping my rather bare poem to blossom. . . . He has just finished the Misadventures of a Chaste Young Man – 64 stanzas (65, M. Bébé calls out!) — obscene and very pretty. Thanks to me Bébé has become obsessed with death in his poems, and thanks to him I have taken on an indecency mania.' The 'rather bare poem' was *Discours du grand sommeil,* a moving work based on his experiences during the war, which he had begun some years earlier and did not publish until 1924. Radiguet's poem, 'The Misadventures of a Chaste Young Man', has never been published.

Cocteau's influence on Radiguet's writing was perhaps never as strong as the influence he claimed to have received, and it was usually indirect. Yet the young man's poems were now consistently more 'classical' in the sense that all typographical experiments had vanished, there were no wasted words, and in contrast to his earlier work the new poems were usually in stanzas of octosyllabic lines and rhymed in a more or less orthodox way. The best aspect of this two-way influence was that when they were together both men worked hard and preserved their own identity.

A reading of Radiguet's poems, and not only those composed during this spring holiday, shows at once that he was preoccupied with imagery from classical mythology, and by one image in particular, that of Venus rising from the sea. He even refers to it in his preface to the poems. Cocteau mentions in the same letter to Valentine Hugo that he and his young friend entertained each other by 'depicting Venus in every conceivable posture' and discussing 'the latest discoveries about her birth and metamorphosis'. A far cry from the poem on which Cocteau was working.

Ultimately, and most important of all, Radiguet's presence brought Cocteau emotional and intellectual stimulus; according to another letter to Valentine Hugo, this holiday was a 'cure' which made up for a year of life at home – in Paris with his mother. He was so happy with 'Bébé' that he did not encourage even his own friends to join them. He was possessive in his happiness. What could be more forgivable? He was in love. In the poems of *Vocabulaire,* published in 1922, he was to tell the world about it.

That 1921 spring 'holiday' increased the output of both writers. Cocteau saw himself as a 'poet' in all fields of creativity, and in the course of his life he practised in almost every medium. Ironically, of his written work, his poetry is now almost totally ignored in favour of the novels and plays. Radiguet's poetry has suffered a similar fate, perhaps more justly: much of it now seems dated and limited. Yet it is fascinating because it provides a key to his psyche and to his apparent potential, which at this stage seemed to have no limits whatever. But he was seemingly not writing love poems to Cocteau. One of the poems he sent to Valentine Hugo, *Les Fiancés de treize ans,* seethes with heterosexual imagery and expresses in its fourteen or so octosyllabic quatrains a *Blé en herbe* situation, with three references to Venus and one to Aphrodite. The poems written during this year were virtually his last and are also regarded as his best. They have retained something of the luminous quality of the seaside light by which he wrote them.

The image of Venus rising from the sea was not kept for his poetry and the literary games with Cocteau. It occurs also in the short story *Denise* which Radiguet wrote at Carqueiranne. The story was never revised and after he wrote it nobody seems to have seen it, except Cocteau, who kept it and a few years later sent it to Daniel Kahnweiler, the art dealer and gallery owner, saying that Radiguet liked him, but not the story. In 1926 it was raised to the dignity of a book, embellished with lithographs by Juan Gris and published by Kahnweiler's Galerie Simon. Cocteau referred to the 'detestably mannered' quality of the story – but he still released it for publication – and told Kahnweiler that he regarded him as the best judge. Death, he said, apparently changes everything, and this story would emphasize the 'purity' of *Le Bal* and show where this purity came from. *Denise* has been included in both editions of the *Oeuvres complètes,* although the Grasset edition has kept it in small print as though to indicate with some disapproval that the story was left unrevised.

In this translation some punctuation has been added and sometimes tenses have been made uniform in an attempt to help the story to run more smoothly. Radiguet might well have disliked the beginning because it shows him making a self-conscious effort – 'I am now writing a short story' – but his sense of humour soon takes over.

DENISE

Paris! From one street corner to another, escaping a pale image reflected from your thousand mirrors – for once I could have wished them less faithful – tell me why I'm lying beneath this pine tree today, waiting for the gardener's daughter. Sailors have come specially from Toulon to carve their hearts and names on these cactus leaves.

In the end I could bear it no longer. Whenever Narcissus had loved too much he would turn away to avoid seeing the reflection of his pallor in the water. As for me, because I haven't cherished my body enough I've been forced to close my eyes in front of every mirror. And if good health seems enviable to me it's thanks to you, resourceful, flourishing roses, I love you today for your cheeks on fire and tomorrow for your callipygousness.

The day I came to this place, where the countryside is both lean and plump like the body of a lovable girl, how impatiently cheerful I was, like a young dog I rushed at the flowers in the fields, biting them, chewing them, keeping them in my mouth for hours, like a sweet which you hope will never dissolve; yet if it didn't, how disappointing, how irritating!

And your fur muffs, beloved hills, where I would bury my head, like a rabbit in his hole. If Denise were naked, I wouldn't treat her more freely. And these flowers whose names suddenly rise from my memory like a jack-in-the-box and then go back again for ever. For hours I sniff about for a scent which I know the flowers don't possess. But sometimes this game can help you to find it in them.

This jasmine smells like English sweets, my nostrils breathe in its pollen until it penetrates my brain. And now, mint or mimosa, you may offer yourselves to me, but you'll both smell of jasmine.

So don't be jealous, Denise, since everything I like is contained in you. If I should like any other girl, it's because I find you in her. And the day before yesterday, when I was waiting for you under our pine tree, and you surprised me innocently embracing that young shepherd, it was your cheeks I was kissing, impatiently. And my pleasure was three-fold, for when you saw me your cheeks turned red.

At last, she's blushed! Like Sister Anne, I'd been waiting; angry with my heart for allowing such a child to play with it, I would venture some movement or word in order to make her blush, and blush on my own. I'd already noticed her lack of reaction on several occasions. As far as bulbs are concerned, the gardener's daughter knows only about narcissus bulbs, they look like onions but they don't make you cry. Denise frightened me; if she hurt her head on a rock no cry escaped her. So impervious to pain, she must be even more so to pleasure.

Courage and cowardice exist only as words. They label our actions, but why give a pejorative meaning to one of them? Since no one rises above himself, it isn't more worthy to be courageous; all our actions are in proportion to ourselves and if I don't cry out on feeling pain either, must I conclude that I'm more courageous than other people? Rather, I'm less sensitive. For me, not being able to cry out at the dentist's is a fault, like not being able to love. But there's a limit to imperviousness in everyone. That's the limit for Denise: seeing me kissing that boy, chastely. Until then she'd felt no pleasure when I kissed her. In her case jealousy came before love, and it's the fact of having seen me kiss someone else that now makes her value *my* kisses.

However, I'm a little disappointed, in spite of my delight, in which the satisfaction of having guessed so much about Denise plays a large part. (How naïve! How stupid! I can't imagine any other explanation for Denise's behaviour. And yet every man would give a different version of it, in his own image, convinced that he alone is right.) Yes, I'm slightly disappointed by the discovery that Denise is not the monster I thought. I ought to know there aren't any monsters, they only exist in relation to ourselves.

And yet I had some cause to regard this girl as a monster. I couldn't succeed in humiliating her and she so much enjoyed humiliating me. Is she like me then, since she enjoys seeing me blush?

I saw her first at her father's, the local nurseryman. I wanted to send some mimosa and red roses to a young Russian girl. I was little inclined to what is called flirting and didn't know exactly what it meant, but I'd been drawn into it all the same. This girl imagined I was paying court to her, merely because she spoke French so badly; in order to understand what she said I had to listen so carefully I seemed to be drinking in her words. So I was angry with this Russian girl for thinking I was flirting with her, and yet it would have been difficult to interpret my attitude in any other way. I was like a little boy who is disgusted by the childishness of some game, such as 'pigeon vole', but plays it, because he's his age after all, and eyes amuse him, even if he despises them.

My pride didn't want to admit that I was in fact flirting. I thought I could easily dispense with the Russian girl; it wasn't so easy though, and I was very glad to find an antidote, Denise. And then the latter, at certain moments when her hand was no longer in mine, felt she was alone in the world, as one suddenly notices at the cinema when a hand takes up the entire screen and turns out to be a whole person in itself.

Due to feeling alone in the world like this, without any aim, my hand wanted to do something which would bring it closer to that Russian girl; such as writing to her or sending her some flowers.

Denise enjoyed my barely concealed anger, for when her mother saw that the basket was addressed to a young girl, the good woman hoped to avoid on my behalf what she considered an error of etiquette, and said to me in horror: 'Oh my goodness! You've sent coloured flowers. You should have sent white carnations to this young lady.'

I was furious that she had dared to give me a lesson in how to behave. I would cheerfully have given her a rude reply but I didn't want that sly girl Denise, who was watching me, to think that a remark of her mother's could have any effect on me. However, I felt a ridiculous need to justify myself; I replied very quickly so that I wouldn't hear the clumsy words:

'Colours have different meanings in different countries. The Chinese wear white for mourning. I don't advise you to send white flowers to a young Russian girl. But there was some point to your remark. I had absent-mindedly allowed you to include a few white carnations.'

She removed them with a sigh; my vanity was saved. I hadn't let her remark go unheeded, and instead of allowing Denise to think that I was unaware of certain customs, I had on the contrary taught her others, which did not exist. Fancy taking so much trouble over a gardener's daughter, I said to myself.

A swimming costume spoilt the pleasure of bathing for me, so I would search out well-hidden places where, in the shelter of the rocks, I could bathe in the nude and then rest in the sun. From time to time I would hear footsteps over my head and then I would use the book I was reading as a fig-leaf. One day I raised my head to look and caught sight of Denise on top of the rock. I hadn't looked at her closely the first time. Her mouth and nose seemed to me much too broad; I realized that they only appeared so because of the particular angle, for since I was lying on my back and looking up with my head thrown back I couldn't see what she was wearing, but I could see her petticoat, and part of her bare thighs above grey silk stockings in which there were several ladders. Her fine brown and rosy complexion, spoilt by that particular shade of mauve flour produced by cheap face powder, her patent leather shoes scratched by pebbles and her tie-silk dress formed a touching ensemble, together with the need to act Parisian, her scorn for the countryside and her parents. The only pleasing detail, which for her must have ruined her appearance, was a basket which if turned upside down would have replaced her respectable hat to advantage. Perhaps it was the sight of her from below, or simply the need for something to do, that made me desire her. As soon as I raised my head she disappeared behind the rocks. I was thinking with some regret that perhaps I would never see her again when she appeared in front of me.

'Excuse me, sir,' she said, smiling, 'which is the way back to Carqueiranne?'

Her nerve astounded me! Daring to ask me to show her a path she must have been taking ever since her childhood. She had come down purely to relish my embarrassment.

'You know better than I do!' I shouted in a very bad temper – bad temper which concealed my embarrassment. She was radiant, and seemed to find it perfectly natural to ask the way, which I realized she knew, from a young man whose only clothing consisted of *The Imitation of Christ*.

'What are you reading? Lend me your book!'

I'd never encountered such a lack of modesty. Was she going to snatch the book from me by force? I shouted at her:

'Be frank at least, you bitch!'

She looked so astonished, with the expression of someone who doesn't understand, that I became a little calmer. But it was too late. I'd already thrown the *Imitation* in her face, feeling silent anger that I couldn't throw the type of book she deserved. She picked the book up with a laugh and ran off, squealing as she went.

Now I regretted what I'd done, and also that I hadn't taken advantage of this girl, who was really easy. A few days later, at the inn where I was staying, I found the *Imitation*, with a letter and a few freshly dried flowers inside it. The sheet of squared paper alone, which had been torn out of a rough notebook, was enough to make me forgive her; I was rather ashamed of my violence, and saw once again that her action had been inspired by shyness.

In her letter Denise indicated the pine tree beneath which she would wait for me that evening, when the dew fell. Apparently she owed me an explanation. I found her beneath the pine, less 'countrylike' than ever. For a moment she was speechless, for I threatened I would never see her again if she disguised herself in this way.

'How do you want me to dress then?' she sighed. She thought I was reproaching her for the bad cut of her dress, and for not being sufficiently Parisian. The prospect of coaching her and leading her astray attracted me more than the pleasure of a love affair.

After accusing her of disguising herself, *I* was disguising her on the pretext of dressing her as someone ought to be dressed in the country.

When desire is rather weak and you want to make it look like love, you must neglect no possibility or detail that occur to the imagination.

If I had not known her, her appearance alone, with the beret that concealed her hair, her sandals, her pullover or her blouse would have been enough to make me turn round to her and covet her. I didn't really know what I expected of Denise. Although ravenous for lips and cheeks, I didn't really enjoy hers very much, appetizing though they were. I preferred fondling the parts of her body that were hidden from sight. On the other hand, since I was too lazy to undress her, I contented myself with kissing her on the breast as far as her fisherman's smock allowed me, and pulling up her dress a little in order to kiss her thighs. We always need to provide explanations for the most unreasonable emotions. And so in order to explain my lack of appetite for her lips, I finally convinced myself that my jealousy was so great that I couldn't love anything about her which she offered to the eyes of the world. However, I had to inflict the most cruel denials on myself. I couldn't understand what was holding me back from possessing Denise. I thought perhaps I was prevented by the fact that she was a virgin. When a man is obstinate, particularly where love is concerned, all is lost. I was convinced that I would make Denise my mistress the day she was no longer a virgin. I wanted someone other than myself to leave her with unpleasant memories. These scruples were to take me a long way. I couldn't explain to myself why I chose the young shepherd-boy whom Denise hated for the task at which I jibbed. I promised him a reward if he succeeded.

So one evening, at the time when I usually met Denise, I sent Dominique to her with a letter. I said I was ill and couldn't come. Dominique found this secret mission fairly entertaining; my motives naturally escaped him.

I sat down near the path and awaited his return with impatience. Whenever anyone went by I ran out, calling Dominique. The postman, an old woman, a man out shooting, it was never him. In the end I went and lurked outside our hiding-place, where they were together. I didn't dare go too close; Denise, far from resisting, seemed to be helping him to accomplish his mission. I went back.

Next day I saw Dominique again. I asked him if Denise had resisted, and what had happened. He lied to me; she had struggled so hard and pleaded with him so earnestly, that he had preferred to make me angry and respect her. I pretended to believe him. I asked Denise, who was equally discreet, no questions. How annoying! To be deceived like this at seventeen, I said to myself, like an old man, and in what circumstances!

My absurd scruples were vanishing: now that I knew she was capable of deceiving me and lying to me so easily, Denise had more value for me. I don't know which one of us I admired in this story, her or myself. Which one had deceived the other more? I knew everything; she would never know that Dominique had made love to her on my orders. I was beginning to be tired of lies. There had to be a few between us, but now we had enough.

It remained for me to teach Denise the pleasure of frankness. However, I didn't dare encourage her to see Dominique again.

As from the day she had allowed him to possess her I felt relieved of a burden. Nothing held me back now; we made love every day, hidden behind the rocks against which her head sometimes fell back in pleasure, as though on a pillow, reminding us of the presence of the sea. Just as a fighter, through the spirit of emulation, fights better in public, old mythologies encouraged me in my love-making with Denise. If by chance Venus emerged from the Mediterranean, she would hope to be loved like this.

We waste our time in regret and hope. In life we are always like a sleepless man in his bed. He thinks he would go to sleep if he slept on his stomach on top of the coverlet, or with his head lower than his feet. This new position satisfies him for a moment, then it seems even more uncomfortable than the others. I had thought I could not possess Denise while she was a virgin; now I was sorry that I had not aroused her body myself. I disliked everything, even the presence of the sea was unbearable to me. I was sorry to think I would soon be returning to Paris, and that I had not once had Denise in my bed.

At last I persuaded her to be rash and come to spend a night with me in my room at the inn. She would return to her parents' home at dawn. At last I would have her completely naked in my arms, nothing would separate our two bodies; at last our horizon would be the walls of a bedroom, and not the sea, which was too big. She was to come at eleven o'clock at night. I left the door of my room ajar, the only light was a night-light. I undressed and waited for her, panting with desire, lying naked on the bed.

Thc cold of that April dawn awokc mc. Grcy light casily makcs bedrooms look like prison cells, and anyone who wakes there looks like a condemned man. As others take communion at this time, I like to smoke a cigarette in order to imagine, before eating, the bitterness this hour must hold for someone about to be guillotined.

I woke with that particular uneasiness that comes when you've thought of something important during the night and you have to remember it. At that moment, as you search through your memory, you suddenly remember something different, the address of a friend, the whereabouts of a wallet you thought you'd lost.

Yes, now Denise was going to come. She didn't come.

I daren't yet believe.... Oh God! I fell asleep before she came.

I tried to calm myself. Surely she didn't come, I'd have woken up. I turned on the light. On the bedside table I found this short note: 'I don't like men who snore. Denise.'

Denise! Denise!

I've never been more bitterly consumed with doubt. The most terrible thing is not knowing what to believe. Women I've loved and whom I suspected of giving themselves to others at the same time; oh yes, that's certainly the case today. How ridiculous my sorrows appear beside that of today.

Denise, I addressed you as *vous,* for all the village boys said *tu* to you; it's not the pleasure of saying *tu* that spurs us on, it's the need to be different from other people. Denise, did I really love you then. I didn't believe one could be so unhappy, but my grief is greater than my love.

To think I'll never know if I really snore.

* * *

More than fifty years have passed since Radiguet wrote this story, and almost as many since it first appeared in a limited edition in France. Critics and commentators have seized upon it hungrily and found it surprisingly nutritious. Radiguet was writing partly for self-entertainment and partly because for the last two years he had been preoccupied with the idea of writing prose, although so far he had completed nothing of any length or depth. He had moved on with giant strides; he still wrote poems, developing his own personal style; he had grown out of any wish to imitate the early surrealists and had become something of a journalist. Yet he had not grown out of his schoolboy interest in the erotic. His poems are full of girls – a cyclist in a trouser-skirt, 'Miss Electricity', 'my beautiful unknown dancer', blushing young girls in white dresses, ondines, Rhine-maidens. He never wrote about them crudely, although they obviously tantalized and embarrassed him. He still hardly knew what to say to them, or even about them: they flit through the poems as though they are not quite real. His own experience was probably more imaginary than he would have liked to admit. His early adventure with Alice, who became the Marthe of *Le Diable au corps,* may not have progressed even half as far as it does in the novel, which was written over a space of about three years, time enough for him to observe and learn, and so add practical details to his half-realized fantasies at the age of sixteen.

Radiguet never wasted a moment of experience. Two incidents from his childhood, both concerning girls, had produced sketches later built into the early part of *Le Diable au corps.* There is no way of knowing if Radiguet met 'Denise' at Carqueiranne – it would hardly have been a success for him if the story really ended the way he wrote it – but in a few lines of prose entitled *Déplacements et villégiatures* he refers to meeting a girl (he calls her Gertrude) when buying Siberian wallflowers. This incident might have been the starting-point for *Denise,* but then again Radiguet might have been embroidering on another early experience, his infatuation as a schoolboy with a girl named Gertrude, whom he pronounced to be his fiancée. It is known that he sent her flowers but, not surprisingly, nothing is known of her response.

Having decided to write an erotic story Radiguet had to look for material. He may even have tried to interest his readers by describing how the narrator was innocently kissing a shepherd boy, to whom he gave the usefully androgynous name of Dominique. The shepherd is apparently just as interested in girls as the narrator, and just as hypocritical. The incident probably has a literary origin: Radiguet admired eighteenth-century novels of all types, he also enjoyed writing parody. The Denise-Dominique incident supplied the hint of a sub-plot in a story that needed some padding.

He writes his way into it with imagery reminiscent of his earlier poems and the delicate paintings of flowers and vegetables he had added to his manuscript for Jacques Doucet. He also introduces a sketch of the narrator-author as a young dog, literally, and the humour of his farcical dialogues for the theatre comes through for a few moments, young, clumsy and forgivable. As he becomes exuberantly preoccupied with his basic erotic theme the tone changes, there is no more nostalgia, no more of Narcissus gazing at his own reflection. Yet Radiguet was doing precisely this, consciously analysing the reasons why he, the narrator, could not seduce Denise at once. Like Marthe in his first novel, like most of the women in Radiguet's life, Denise makes the first advances. Like most of these women too she brings out that streak of cruelty so clear in *Le Diable au corps,* so usual in a very young man and so much a part of Radiguet. He almost always got his own way, with both women and men, and people found themselves obediently doing what he wanted them to do. In a strange way, they sensed that if they 'disobeyed' him they would suffer.

His narrator feels no love for Denise, only lust; he wants to possess her and in particular to lead her astray; he is attracted by her anger and jealousy. Yet at the same time he cannot sustain a superficial approach, if that is what he is trying to do. The much-quoted Radiguet aphorisms begin to appear, he indulges in those moralizing sentences which lend surprising maturity to his two novels. French critics have pointed out these 'judgements' in *Denise*: the remarks about courage, or the need to work out the reasons behind unreason. It is surely this quality that led Cocteau to allow publication of the story. At its best this piece of prose allows us to see the author of the novels developing, and at its worst it shows the muddled faults of a young writer who, it should be remembered, was presumably a partner in some form of sex life with Cocteau while at the same time rarely taking his eyes off the girls.

The reference to *The Imitation of Christ* as the fig-leaf book would have struck Cocteau as essentially poor taste, but he in his turn never forgot the pleasures of bathing in the nude by isolated sunny beaches, writing about them in *Le Livre blanc* and recalling a young man he had loved, who 'had many women friends', and is clearly identifiable as Radiguet.

Nor would Cocteau have found the figure of Denise particularly interesting or amusing, but through Radiguet's descriptions of her we can see how the suburban schoolboy had developed. He does not tell us the colour of her eyes or her hair, but we know how she dressed and how she tried pathetically to look sophisticated and 'Parisian'. Radiguet in Paris had become something of a dandy – he could hardly have escaped the influence of Cocteau and his friends in this respect – and was already accustomed to the company of women who were fashionably or exotically dressed. His poems show an awareness of women's clothes and when he added drawings of women to his manuscripts he added an element of nostalgia, they are wearing nineteenth-century crinolines and carrying sunshades.

This would-be erotic story, 'detestably mannered' or not, amusing and intriguing because Radiguet wrote it, revealing because he put so much of himself into it, will pass a few moments for the reader on a sunny beach, just as Radiguet passed a few hours writing it. For once the heroine has the last word and the hero is, to say the least, discomfited. The story, which seems to ask for a film camera, has one thing in common with Radiguet's two novels – he was particularly fascinated by the moment when love or desire begins, less so by what happens next, and was forced to end his story with a moment of drama. On this occasion the 'drama' is a joke, and no commentator should pretend it is anything else.

At the end of May 1921, three extraordinary theatrical matinées took place at the Théâtre Michel in Paris. There were five items on the programme, described as a *spectacle de théâtre bouffe,* and the name of Raymond Radiguet was the only one to appear twice. None of the works presented have achieved world fame, although their creators were and remain well known. The performances were organized by the actor Pierre Bertin, who produced the show, acted in it and earned Cocteau's praise for his courage and his financial investment – for the whole programme was aimed at a specialist audience and was unlikely to make anyone's fortune.

The first item was *La Femme fatale* by Max Jacob, 'a lyrical drama in one act' in which, according to Cocteau, poetic parody and true poetry were mingled. Unfortunately the text has been lost, but Bertin at least has described it as 'very chivalric'. Then came *Le Piège de Méduse,* a 'lyrical comedy in one act by Monsieur Erik Satie, with music for dancing by the same gentleman'. There was no libretto for the third item, a 'shimmy for jazz band' by Darius Milhaud, performed by the Negro dancer Graton.

It was followed by the most substantial piece in a not very solid programme, *Les Pélican,* a play in two acts by Raymond Radiguet with music by Georges Auric. This was the play Radiguet had written the previous year, the only work for the theatre that he completed (his revue sketches were not written for production and his other work for the theatre was done in collaboration with Cocteau). It was Cocteau himself who gave the most telling description of it, two years later, in a talk to the Collège de France on the theme *Order considered as Anarchy.* He referred to the 'astonished audience' and added his own opinion of the play: 'I have never seen a soap bubble blown up so far without bursting.'

We have already considered *Les Pélican* in some detail, but it is worth mentioning here an insight of Nadia Odouard's, that indefatigable analyst of Radiguet's personality. She has pointed out how far he endowed the play's characters with aspects of himself and his own behaviour: Parfait is short-sighted; the governess likes reading; Anselme is considered hopeless at school work; and Hortense contemplates suicide, as Radiguet is thought to have done at least once.

Cocteau also remembered Radiguet's behaviour at the theatre. 'After the play,' he said, 'the alarming author walked the corridors in order to embarrass well-informed people who didn't know what to say to him.' Should they discuss literary or dramatic points with the seventeen-year-old playwright? Should they laugh with him, or at him? No one knew. The play caused enough interest, however, to earn publication the same year by the Galerie Simon, embellished with seven etchings by Henri Laurens, and in 1951 it was performed again in Paris, in a 'choreographic production' devised by Jean-Jacques Etcheverry.

The programme at the Théâtre Michel ended with a piece called *Le Gendarme incompris* to which no author's name was added. This was the anti-Mallarmé piece which Cocteau and Radiguet had worked on the previous year, finishing it at Le Picquey when Cocteau's bad cold left Radiguet sitting outside his room on the balcony. It occupies eighteen pages in the second of the *Cahiers Jean Cocteau,* where it was first published in 1971. Its plot is a complete absurdity. Monsieur Médor, a provincial *commissaire de police,* complains that business has lapsed and nothing has happened since the Dreyfus affair. He meditates about his social aspirations and reveals how he would like to dine at the local château where a Dreyfus supporter is in fact a guest that evening. Suddenly he has clients. A creature apparently dressed as a priest is brought in by the *gendarme* and accused of shocking masturbatory behaviour – a 'chaste frenzy'. The *gendarme,* whose name, remarkably, is La Pénultième, makes his report in pompous, near-incomprehensible language. The accused is found to be no priest, but the eccentric chatelaine herself. The *commissaire,* ready for blackmail, arranges to release her provided he is invited to dinner. The unfortunate *gendarme* is accused of disrespect, threatened with disciplinary action, and that is all. Poulenc had composed five musical numbers, said to be delightful, and the audience found the whole thing ridiculous.

Georges Auric has described how afterwards the co-authors of this piece, together with Jean and Valentine Hugo, joined him at a *café terrasse* to hold a post-mortem. Poulenc had gone home, feeling depressed no doubt, for the group of friends had been particularly optimistic about this last item. Cocteau had even hoped to equal the success of *Le Boeuf sur le Toit.* The sad fact was that the elaborate literary joke had fallen flat, and he was forced to explain the joke, the anti-Mallarmé skirmish. He found his chance to reply in the magazine *Comoedia,* after the newspapers had published their reviews. He said that 'during their two hours of work' the co-authors were not aware of setting a trap and had done so 'without the slightest malice'. He was sorry to inform various critics that '*Le Gendarme* is a criticism, in the sense that it is motivated by the Stéphane Mallarmé style, and that this criticism is farcical because it laughs at itself at the same time, while its novelty arises from the fact that instead of commenting on a text it merely shows it from a new angle.' The policeman La Pénultième ('was his name not a sign?') pronounces no single word which does not come, without the slightest alteration, from the famous *L'Ecclésiastique* in Mallarmé's *Divagations.*

He pointed out that the *commissaire* had even mentioned a later and better version of the sonnet he had recited, Mallarmé's famous *Placet futile,* and went on to say that the critics would be no less surprised to learn that *Le Gendarme* was only a literary game, that several characters had Mallarmian names and that the entire plot was conducted 'by allusions to writing that any man concerned with literature should recognize immediately'. He could not resist quoting the critic who had written in *Le Figaro* that 'the alembicated palinodes of this stupid copper are only too comprehensible to a modest old Parisian like me'. 'Poor Mallarmé!' wrote Cocteau, would he ever recover? He added that he would not be cruel to critics for in Paris, '*qui juge beaucoup, écoute peu*'.

This was Paris at the beginning of the 'twenties. The previous year Valéry had published *Le Cimetière marin* and critics had hardly been kind to him. People had found it more amusing to talk about the Bar Gaya, later to become famous as Le Boeuf sur le Toit, more dramatic to reflect on the death of Modigliani. In 1921 there occurred two theatrical events of value, the production of Cocteau's *Les Mariés de la Tour Eiffel* and the more far-reaching *Six Characters in Search of an Author.* Yet Cocteau, who worried more about failure than he would ever admit, was desperately anxious to explain that he and Radiguet at least knew their Mallarmé. Radiguet had already said his say about *Les Divagations* in *Règle du jeu,* but of course it had not been completed, let alone published. It is not clear who chose the passage from *L'Ecclésiastique,* but Cocteau himself used the final version of the famous Mallarmé sonnet in his late play *L'Impromptu du Palais-Royal.* His touch was less farcical than Radiguet's, kinder on the whole. Ironically enough Radiguet's poetry has since been compared to that of Mallarmé and several years later Cocteau became a member of the Académie Mallarmé. The older poet, who had died in 1898, had grown in stature by then and still continues to do so, new commentaries on his work appear every year, each one more stimulating and less conclusive than the last.

On the surface at least 1921 looked like another year of holidays and theatrical entertainment for Cocteau and Radiguet. Yet holidays, especially by the sea, produced writing, and afternoons or evenings at the theatre gave Radiguet experience as a playwright – of a kind – and sounder experience as a critic. This same year saw the publication by the Editions de la Sirène, Cocteau's firm, of another group of poems, called *Devoirs de vacances,* literally 'holiday tasks', with three drawings by Irène Lagut, an artist and stage designer about whom Radiguet had written a piece in *Littérature* two years earlier. Apparently she was one of the young man's growing band of female admirers and her fulsome letters to him have been preserved in the Cocteau archives. Of Radiguet's attitude to her nothing is known and it was no doubt standard – he admired the artist, liked the woman, accepted her admiration and cared no further.

Cocteau of course cared still more deeply for his young friend and they were constantly together. He did not neglect his many other friends and he continued to show an affectionate interest in André Gide's young protégé Marc Allégret, who later made his name in the film world. However, Radiguet preoccupied him utterly and when they were not actually collaborating, mainly for their own entertainment, they were working on their own separate projects, but constantly discussing them, exchanging ideas and sometimes hardly knowing who might have said or written something first and who might have echoed it. Yet many people saw Radiguet as longing to be on his own, or at least to be able to escape temporarily from Cocteau. He needed the older man and wished he didn't. Probably this led to the tension that made him drink too much and explains why, on one occasion at least, he made a token rebellion by refusing to leave a dinner-party when Cocteau left, assuming his friend would accompany him. Radiguet knew Cocteau was anxious about the success of *Les Mariés de la Tour Eiffel* and chose this moment to irritate him. Radiguet's eighteenth birthday, on 18 June, coincided with the production of the *comédie-ballet,* the end of a busy theatrical season. The Dadaists took this opportunity to demonstrate against Cocteau and only after a week of performances could he feel pleased with the reception for this complex work which seemed so fragile, its superficial lightness preventing many people from realizing its true novelty.

Whatever Radiguet's feelings about Cocteau the man, he had nothing but praise for the writer. But he had to wait eight months before his article about *Les Mariés* was published in *Les Feuilles libres.* It was no mere review, although all the collaborators in the work received a well-turned compliment. Radiguet referred to several other writers, mostly French classics, and to one of Cocteau's verse collections. He seized the essence of the work: 'For the first time, thanks to Jean Cocteau, we are given a play where poetry is expressed theatrically.' There was no obvious 'poetic' style in *Les Mariés:* 'the language is not full of imagery, but the play itself is.' The work could only be mentioned, he wrote, in the same context as Molière, the Greek tragedians and fairy stories. It was a long way from Alfred Jarry's *Ubu roi,* and Cocteau had the gift of 'endowing the things of today with an ancient mythological character (the only way of giving them some freshness). . . .' Ronsard had perpetuated the beauty of his mistresses in poetry, Cocteau, by means of poetry, had made the Eiffel Tower look beautiful for ever.

The review ended with remarks which clarified Radiguet's own personal and critical position, using heterosexual imagery and attacking the members of the avant-garde who liked crude descriptions: 'Our lovers of raw meat reproach Cocteau for having scaled down the object of their affection. No doubt: a woman encountered in the street can give us a kind of pleasure whose violence is different from that we feel in the company of a beloved mistress.' Life was not a perpetual Luna Park of amusements and attractions. After a quick stab at the Dadaists he concluded: 'But what good fortune, when you can guess, on seeing a new face, that you will never tire of it. A truly bourgeois ideal, no doubt, but fortunately it is mine.'

Did the *comédie-ballet* really deserve such praise? the present-day reader or theatre-goer will ask. Radiguet was not too wide of the mark: without *Les Mariés* there might never have been Anouilh or Ionesco.

When Radiguet wrote like this, indeed when he wrote at all, Cocteau forgave him everything and did his best to take him away from Paris as often as he could. In the summer of 1921 Radiguet did not settle down to holidays immediately, but this may well have been Cocteau's fault, for when they left the city they took its atmosphere with them, travelling with a group of Paris friends. They went first to Besse-en-Chandesse in the Auvergne, partly to be near

Issoire where Georges Auric often stayed. They were unlucky enough to encounter the heavy rain for which this unspoilt area of France is famous. The inhabitants have always had a poor reputation and the Parisians found them unwelcoming and dirty. Radiguet is said to have behaved badly, no one knows exactly in what way, and Cocteau forgave him again, explaining to the others that his young friend was still an adolescent. Not that the behaviour of the party as a whole was particularly adult during the first part of that holiday, but it may have been the bad weather that forced them to play indoor theatrical games and act an impromptu play called *La Famille Musset* in which Cocteau took the part of the Romantic poet Alfred de Musset, Auric became George Sand and Radiguet a Hindu servant – to what effect has not been recorded.

It was not long before the friends returned to Le Picquey. Here Cocteau felt at home. Radiguet's visit the previous year had been all too brief and he had had no time to absorb the atmosphere of this remarkable place. They stayed again at the little hotel with wooden balconies, Le Chantecler. It was run by 'la mère Dourthe' who liked writers but had no intention of running a charitable institution for them. Her rates were not cheap.

The area had been a fashionable place for working holidays, retreat and escape. On the other side of the basin was Le Moulleau, where in the past Gabriele d'Annunzio had stayed to avoid his creditors. From there too he had issued the appeal to his fellow countrymen which was at least partly responsible for Italy's entry into the war in 1916. The villages and small hotels were isolated, natives and tourists travelled in boats, called *pinasses,* or walked by way of the beaches. According to Jean Hugo, the baker drove round in a horse-drawn cart, preferring the shallow water where the sand was harder. Hugo, a close friend of Radiguet and Cocteau, has written a memorable description of the area: 'No place in France resembles the western shore of the bassin d'Arcachon as it was then: a place without soil, without stones, without paths; only sand, transparent water, pine forests, wooden huts. In the middle of the bassin was the Ile aux Oiseaux, whose oyster beds at low tide resembled miniature towns of lake dwellings, at high tide only a line of points indicated their presence; in the distance, a mountain of snow, Fuji Yama of this Japanese landscape, the large Le Pyla dune. At the end of the day sky, water and sand were the same pink: you felt you were inside a pearl.'

It was the ideal place for a working holiday, and during this year of so-called holidays Radiguet 'grew up'; he almost settled down to prose-writing. Both Cocteau and Jacques Doucet had urged him to write prose at least two years earlier and he had started a novel of sorts in 1919, probably writing the preliminary sketches which later formed the beginning of *Le Diable au corps.* Now he changed his whole life-style, drinking milk instead of alcohol, but the settling-down process hardly happened overnight. He wanted to work but, as Cocteau wrote later, he was 'torn between the certainty of writing something marvellous and the moodiness of a lazy schoolboy'. Cocteau found that the best way to persuade him to work was in fact to treat him like a schoolboy and lock him in his room; 'he used to escape through the window, and if he had promised to write he would scribble something, just anything, in illegible handwriting.' Then there might be a change of attitude: 'Afterwards he would behave like a Chinese sage, rolling cigarettes, bending over exercise books until his face touched them, and giving the impression that he was a good scholar, a grave and conscientious writer. The outcome of these alternating moods and the long gaps during which he lived in terrifying chaos was to be a masterpiece of French literature: *Le Diable au corps.'*

Radiguet left Le Picquey that autumn with over a hundred pages of his novel completed. Cocteau, who had been writing *Le Secret professionnel,* was excited about the manuscript and felt that his belief in the young man was now more than justified.

If Radiguet enjoyed the luminous unreality of Le Picquey, if he too felt that he had been 'inside a pearl', none of this poetic, romantic quality found its way into his novel. As the starting-point for his simple plot he had gone back to his relationship with Alice in 1917. In the early draft of the novel he even kept her name, but later it was changed to 'Marthe'. The narrator meets Marthe, whose fiancé, later her husband, is at the front. The young 'hero', still a schoolboy living through the holiday of the war, adopts unconsciously attitudes which have spilled over into civilian life from the war itself: he observes coldly, he behaves ruthlessly when he has to, or even when he feels like it. His only confidant is his father. As he spends more time with Marthe, he comes to dominate her existence, persuading her to buy furniture that he likes. He experiences all the moods of a shared sexual life; temporarily he desires another girl, at the same time still wanting Marthe for himself; he notes how sexual enjoyment and love can fall apart. But how was the story to end? When Radiguet came back to Paris in the autumn he still did not know.

In Paris there were other stories, other relationships, and these were now causing problems. Cocteau, still omnipresent, quickly sold the rights of the unfinished novel to the Editions de la Sirène and was then forced to spend what he called an 'atrocious' winter trying to make his protégé go on writing. But Radiguet rebelled, frequently trying to escape Cocteau's discipline. With the money he had received from the publishing firm he bought expensive pigskin luggage – was escape so much on his mind? – and good quality clothes.

1922

The most spectacular of Radiguet's escapes, from Paris and from Cocteau, has been described by the British painter Nina Hamnett; although it is probably only partly accurate her account makes a good story. In January 1922, a few days before the official opening of the bar Le Boeuf sur le Toit, Nina Hamnett, accompanied by Radiguet and the Roumanian-born sculptor Brancusi, arrived at the Montparnasse café, Le Dôme, at about five to two in the morning, 'just in time to buy some cigarettes'. Radiguet was wearing a dinner jacket, often *de rigueur* at the time for various social occasions, including visits to the theatre, and in any case he was something of a dandy now and liked formal clothes, especially since the 'bohemians' didn't. Brancusi suggested suddenly that they should all go to Marseilles. Radiguet said yes, Nina Hamnett no, and regretted it for the rest of her life. The whole point of the trip was to go that very minute, out of devilment, away from Cocteau and all the Montparnasse circle. The two men left Paris by train later that morning, Radiguet still wearing his dinner jacket.

At Marseilles he went to a sailor's shop and outfitted himself for a seaside holiday. He wrote telegrams and postcards to various friends and then accepted Brancusi's second suggestion: having come so far they might as well travel a little farther and take the boat to Corsica. They stayed in Corsica for a fortnight, as long as their money lasted, while the agitated and jealous Cocteau waited for news in Paris. Ten years later he found the courage to remember the incident in *Le Livre blanc,* changing only the names. 'One morning I received a telegram: "Don't worry. Have left on a trip with Marcel. Will telegraph time return."' And a little later: 'I received telegrams: "Long live Marseilles!" or "Leaving for

Tunis".' According to Nina Hamnett the two men had 'a wonderful time with the peasants and the Corsican brandy'.

Someone who had once thanked Radiguet for a card from Marseilles, although grumbling at the same time, was a woman called Beatrice Hastings. He had probably met her through Brancusi, who had a great many friends and was popular because he would cook peasant-style food for them. Radiguet lived mainly in hotels now, either on his own or close to Cocteau. He seemed to look for the semblance of a home atmosphere and as part of this quest as well as part of his escape from Cocteau he also looked for women.

1917 and the romantic weeks with Alice now seemed long ago. Since then Radiguet had obviously found many admiring women or, to be more accurate, they had found him. Despite his fantasies about young girls, they were usually older than him. He did not want love; he was glad to have admiration, help with his work, intellectual stimulus, sexual adventures – but love, emotional demands, no. Radiguet the novelist eventually knew a great deal about love, but how far he met it in his own life is not clear. His poems are full of the girls he desired and enjoyed, but if men and women loved him, nobody, not even Cocteau, kept his affection. Cocteau said once that you needed a diamond to scratch his heart. Radiguet was hardly handsome, but he caught the eye. By the time he was eighteen he was less disfigured by untidy hair and inadequate spectacles. He intrigued and attracted by his distant, disapproving air, he was painted and sketched, sculpted by Lipschitz, photographed by Man Ray. Yet because he was still developing so fast, none of the portraits in whatever medium look the same. Dark hair, large eyes, 'like almonds,' said Cocteau, a full sensuous mouth which often looked sulky. And if Madame Cocteau had disliked his manners when she first met him, they had improved. To women he was now excessively polite, when it suited him, and he had a gift for making them laugh.

Women noticed him and as for his response, he showed a preference for foreigners. During 1921 and 1922 he may well have regretted it. No doubt Radiguet knew something about Beatrice Hastings, for everyone knew about her liaison with Modigliani, which had begun in the summer of 1914. She was older than the painter but her life story was hardly less strange. She had been born in Port Elizabeth, South Africa, in 1879 and is said to have married a 'pugilist' called Hastings. No one was sure about her family name but the family realized early in her life that they must send this eccentric young woman a long way away and keep her away by means of an allowance. She went to London, probably by way of New York. Her artist and writer friends in Paris knew her later as the 'English poetess' and described her fantastic clothes and accessories: she would dress like an eighteenth-century shepherdess, wear hats with long ribbons and even carry a crook and a basket full of live ducks.

She did indeed write poetry, took up a variety of causes, such as feminism, and rushed backwards and forwards between emotional and ideological extremes. In London she worked and lived with Alfred Orage, editor of the well-known literary magazine *The New Age.* She helped him publish the great names current at the time and more important still, helped him to find the new ones like Ezra Pound and Havelock Ellis. With Beatrice's help Katherine Mansfield published early work in the magazine and, again with her help, had an abortion in 1910. Their friendship dissolved when Beatrice became jealous of her relationship with John Middleton Murry. Soon afterwards the exhausting South African left London for Paris, where she spent her time with writers and artists, writing about them for *The New Age.* Orage obviously preferred her to be on the other side of the Channel. She became Modigliani's mistress; an uncomfortable life, but she survived even Modigliani's violence. He painted her often and she is said to have had a good influence on him; certainly she understood his painting and sculpture at a time when many others didn't. But after two years even she had had enough, and before Modigliani turned briefly to Simone Thiroux she had begun a secret liaison with a handsome, but not very interesting sculptor called Alfredo Pina.

For a time no lovers, eminent or otherwise, were recorded. Beatrice filled her time travelling, writing and deciding that she was a medium.

There is no record of where she met Radiguet. A dozen or so

letters she wrote to him, and a letter and a long poem she wrote to Cocteau, document what must have been an exhausting relationship for all three. The affair was short-lived but it is worth considering in some detail for the light it throws on Radiguet's attitude towards and treatment of women, and on the relationship between Radiguet and Cocteau.

At first, addressing him as *vous,* she sent Radiguet two hundred pages of a novel she had written, saying that if he could do it better she would give him her copyright. Then, calling him *tu,* she implored him not to show her letters to Auric. The composer, whom Radiguet liked very much, was afraid that Cocteau would discover that he had been involved in introducing Radiguet to a woman. Beatrice was quick to tell Radiguet what she felt about him. She could not exist without drama: 'When you've really killed me I'll become a nun. I'm dying from not seeing you. I'm impatient for the *coup de grâce.*' Immediately there was intrigue. 'Cocteau (don't betray me!) tells me you take *le rôle ignoble,*' she wrote. But Radiguet could do no wrong. She was mad about him. 'I kiss you on . . . hard to choose when everything is perfect. . . . Lord! How I'd like to have you here to laugh a little.' But the problem of individual reputations in this sexual jungle was a serious one and she worried about it. Radiguet seems to have tired of her quickly – she was, after all, more than twice his age – but she was not easy to shake off. Modigliani was said to have been afraid of her, but she seems to have met her match in Radiguet; unfortunately for him, this made her all the more determined to win and keep him. He adopted the same tactics as he used to escape from Alice, arriving late or not at all. But he could not prevent her from writing letters, and even kept some of them.

Into these letters she poured all her violent feelings, apparently determined to prove that although Radiguet had spurned her, she was by no means destroyed. 'Is the menagerie complete now,' she asked, 'since you've brought out the viper? I was quite ready for it, since no respectable jungle is without one of these nasty little creatures. And it tried to bite in accordance with its nature, from behind.' Did her lover leave an unkind note? Presumably. 'You cross Paris at night to be with me . . . and when I hold out my hands to you and my entire heart, not to mention a shoulder against which you sleep very well – then you run away leaving a little hissing snake instead. I'd like to ask you what's the matter with you, but would you be capable of answering me? But I don't because if you don't believe I love you more than anyone in the world no explaining on my part could convince you. . . . It's enough for me that when I see you I want to kiss you at once, and you don't seem to want me to languish at all! . . .

'I want you to know this very evening that the viper hasn't killed me.

'I love you all the same.

'Come soon.'

She complained he had not replied, worried in case he had taken things tragically; he must never be *solennel,* she said. Then she tried to unravel an impossibly complicated situation. She went to see Cocteau and told him about the relationship between herself and Radiguet. Cocteau was in a desperate state and was ready to beat Radiguet, apparently because he feared that his friend was involved with other *men.* She had told Cocteau partly 'to stop him thinking he has such rights'. There had been a rumour that Radiguet and Brancusi had had a sexual relationship and only her existence could prove that Radiguet had not been unfaithful to Cocteau with other men. She was sorry for Cocteau but he was '*passablement méchant*' and very tortuous. Cocteau told her that Radiguet did not want to see her but she refused to believe it. 'It's because you're furious and stupid,' she wrote to her young lover. 'I avoid going where I might see you because you're never as handsome as you are at my place.'

It is possible to identify Beatrice with the 'Mademoiselle R' in *Le Livre blanc,* the woman who comes to tell the narrator that his lover, H, had in fact loved *her.* One would like to believe that Cocteau did not beat Radiguet as he threatened to do, but there is a horribly violent scene in *Le Livre blanc*: 'I flung Mademoiselle R's name at him. He denied it. I insisted. He denied it. I bullied him. He denied it. Finally he admitted it and I hit him. Pain intoxicated me. I beat him like a brute.' Surely Cocteau is exaggerating, but the fact that he wrote this at all proves the degree of his jealousy, whatever his lover's sexual preferences.

If Beatrice had not had such a capacity for anger one might almost feel sorry for her. Cocteau had taken care to explain that she had only seen one aspect of Radiguet, '*une grimace*', and that Radiguet's pleasures were variable. Cocteau even advised him to answer her letters, advice which she considered ungallant and stupid. Writing her novel had tired her, she told him, and she would go on writing her poem about him, it was going to be fairly long and perhaps in the end it would make her tear up her novel.

Radiguet was about to go away but since most of these letters are undated the trip cannot be identified. Beatrice indicates that she refused to go (with Brancusi? with Cocteau?) and Radiguet went instead. In spite of her fury she could still laugh nastily for a moment: '[I] had to console myself by thinking of the two of you sitting on a rock in the moonlight and each thinking how delightful it would be if Beatrice were here.'

But Beatrice was not there and even if she went to Le Picquey briefly it is unlikely that she enjoyed herself. When Radiguet came back to Paris she turned her jealousy on someone else, Marie Beerbohm, the daughter of Sir Julius Beerbohm and one of the many friends of Nina Hamnett. Radiguet had been seen with her and Beatrice accused Marie of flaunting her conquest of him, just to infuriate *her*, and could not bear to think that her former lover had accepted such a situation. 'I'm all the more upset because for my novel I need to write very tenderly about you at the moment. I beg you as a writer to leave me some illusion. I've no intention of quarrelling over you with her or anybody. I can't do anything for you.' Literature in the end was the only thing that mattered. 'I've begun to write a realistic novel in your style where life and truth triumph in spite of personal opinions – that is how realism has its revenge for the evil I've said about it. It's in this way that from one point of view Jean Cocteau will emerge as completely *sympathique*. Too bad, I'll have a mass said for his recovery. As for you, you'll be very pleased because you'll have a rather unpleasant part. If you were nice you would enlighten me on some points that my deepest comprehension of unpleasantness leaves obscure.' She told him to have a good time with his 'Jewess with Venus-like legs' and to leave her in peace.

In December 1921 Beatrice was still so obsessed with the relationship between Cocteau and Radiguet, which, of course, she had complicated still further, that she wrote a poem about it. She addressed this extraordinary piece – twenty-five quatrains in rhymed alexandrines – to Cocteau, sending Radiguet a copy. She continued her zoological metaphor in a letter: 'When you're alone with me, you resemble a man – with animal-like divergences, it's true – and also an angel of grace and tenderness.' As soon as other people were concerned he behaved like an animal. 'I've already seen a fierce bear, a pitiless tiger and a badly behaved, perfidious, destructive monkey. I'm vastly intrigued wondering what monster you will let out next.' Every time she had tried to help him he had made mistakes and been foolish. But she had recovered. 'Last Tuesday afternoon I was unfaithful to you just to see, and as I enjoyed it very much I decided that you were completely in the wrong. O ornament of the French race, when will you come to help me with Narcissus? I love you so much when you're nice!'

The poem she sent to Cocteau was not nice, but it was not unkind. Most of all it was sad, for she had loved and lost. She seems to have been convinced that Radiguet loved her, which he surely did not. The poem is full of contrasts – despairing romantic imagery contrasting with casual references to Max Jacob and Georges Auric. In a sense, the whole thing was laughable. But Beatrice had to write the poem as an attempt to express everything she felt and to inform Cocteau and anyone else interested that she had withdrawn from the fight. She didn't want anyone to feel sorry for her, but she announced with would-be tragic dignity that she cared for both men, that all three of them were in love but unable to communicate, and all three deserved her tears:

Je vous envoie ce mot. Je vous aime tous deux.
J'erre dans le désert... Je songe avec effroi.
A nos coeurs sourds, muets, aveugles, amoureux.
Je sais que chacun aime – et je pleure tous trois.

She also wrote to Cocteau and told him that Radiguet had never said a word against him. Other people also received confused letters and they in turn wrote to Cocteau asking him to explain.

The 'atrocious' winter wore on and Radiguet's novel was still not finished. Cocteau tried hard to make him work but the author was unable to finish the story; perhaps he felt too close to the narrator, who superficially at least seemed to be living through so much of his own experience. He struggled on with the book, staying with friends at Fontainebleau, arguing with Cocteau, throwing re-written pages into the fire, then admitting later that Cocteau's advice had been right. Cocteau believed that Radiguet had been influenced by friends encountered at La Rotonde, an Englishman and an American woman, and the influence had not been good. However, the book had been improved so much that Cocteau realized he could arrange a better publishing deal than the one he had concluded in the autumn. He had a talk with Bernard Grasset, the publisher, who had successfully published an edition of the posthumous first novel by Louis Hémon, *Maria Chapdelaine,* now a minor classic. Grasset wanted to follow it up with something equally sensational and when Cocteau brought the manuscript of *Le Diable au corps,* and its author, to his office, he was certain he had found it. Cocteau read parts of the manuscript aloud to him, while Radiguet said not a word and behaved like a schoolboy who had been sent to see the headmaster, Grasset remembered afterwards.

He saw Radiguet's problems, gave him editorial advice and arranged to pay him a monthly salary. Radiguet did not pay back the advance he had already received from the Editions de la Sirène – no doubt he had already spent it all, indulging his own tastes but also sending money to his family, whom he never forgot, even if he saw them less often. Gradually the worst of his problems seemed to be nearing solution. Nothing had been heard from Beatrice Hastings since a New Year note wishing him all the best for 1922. Nothing is known about his adventures with Marie Beerbohm, who seems to have been undemanding, and at the beginning of May he left with Cocteau for the south. When they came back, in November, both men had written a great deal and it looked as though Radiguet's literary career was fully mapped out.

Working at Le Grand Hôtel at Le Lavandou it took Radiguet only a few days to finish his novel. He found a simple solution to the problem of how to end the book: his heroine had to die. No fewer than five manuscript versions of the ending of *Le Diable au corps* have been preserved, but the published one is simple: Marthe dies after giving birth to a son, who is, of course, the child of the narrator. The finality of this ending seems to show Radiguet's determination to break away from his past and from the book which had occupied him since 1919. The writing at least was over, publication was not scheduled until the following year. Controversy about the 'story behind the story' would then begin, and indeed has not yet come to an end.

In the meantime Radiguet had no intention of having more than a short rest. He had been thinking about a second book for some time and here at Le Lavandou there was nothing to distract him from writing. Cocteau too was hard at work; he apparently wrote the whole of his novel *Le Grand Ecart* between 15 and 19 June, remembering his teenage *affaires* with girls and boys. Admittedly it was short, but he had never written a novel before, even if *Le Potomak* has always been listed as the first entry in his *poésie du roman.* Who was the first to say, *'Il faut faire des romans comme tout le monde'*? Cocteau or Radiguet? No matter, but it is significant that Cocteau began to write novels while he was close to Radiguet and wrote only one, *Les Enfants terribles,* after his death.

It was probably during the early summer at Le Lavandou that Radiguet wrote the two prose pieces entitled *Carnets I* and *II.* Cocteau told his mother that Radiguet divided his time between sleeping and writing a story. Admittedly the 'story' could have been any of the unfinished pieces which were later published in the Club des Libraires edition of the complete works, and only half of this piece is the beginning of a narrative, but everything suggests that it was written at this time. The *Carnets,* or 'Notebooks', starting with would-be sophisticated notes about Montparnasse, and ending with memories of melodramatic incidents from his childhood, tell us a great deal about Radiguet himself, despite their confused grammar.

NOTEBOOKS

Notebook I

At the end of the war Montparnasse was not as it is today. Now, thanks to Cook's travel agency, tourists go to La Rotonde in motor coaches. After the success of the new religion, the crèche, where a layer of straw concealed a good deal of manure, has become a cathedral. The rare tourists exhausted by Rheims Cathedral. . . . And when you see them filing past, they almost take their hats off – keep your hats on, my friends – going through the cafés to stop, at the right distance, in front of hideous paintings, just as people admire stained glass windows, the drinkers seated at the tables – visitors and drinkers get in each others' way – all feel uneasy. The drinkers interrupt their discussions about the fourth dimension just as the inhabitants of a historic château would feel obliged to interrupt a violent family discussion in front of the troop of sightseers. As at Fontainebleau: 'It was here, ladies, in this gallery and at this table that Napoleon signed the act of abdication', at La Rotonde you always expect to hear, by a marble table: 'It was here that so-and-so renounced cubism. It was here that Modigliani. . . .'

Sometimes, but rarely, the tourists are lucky enough to see a reconstruction like they have at the Musée Grévin: Some former habitués of La Rotonde round a table. The day when the new Rotonde was opened everyone had this feeling in fact. That opening was a funeral. Old habitués, who could be seen a few years earlier in *sabots* and pullovers, got out of their cars and shook hands with people who had remained what they had been a few years earlier, so much so that some of them must have had the curious feeling of seeing themselves in a mirror as they had been a few years earlier.

Picasso, who is always ahead of everyone, was the first to understand that Montparnasse was dead. From 1917 onwards he was no longer seen at La Rotonde even when the excitement was at its height. It will certainly go on, to untrained eyes, but it was only the last twitches of a dying animal that made people think it was still alive.

A duck whose head has been cut off goes on walking for a short time, and without quoting more tragic examples from among those who went to the war, many people have seen a soldier hit by a shell turn into a soldier without a head, and take a couple of steps before falling. When it lost Picasso, Montparnasse lost its head.

But just as when the light of a star reaches us that star is in fact dead, Montparnasse has never looked so alive as when it is dead. And there is nothing to regret. Young people laugh at reconstructions. The Montparnasse period was concerned with inventions. Far from telling each other about their work, people concealed it carefully. They fought over each other's patents. For a whole week it was whispered that So-and-So had invented *a new way of doing trees* etc . . . etc. . . . However, there is every excuse for those who live in the past. Let us hope that what such specialists from the heroic age regret is not the age itself but their own lost youth. It is their only excuse. Apollinaire, who believed in prophecies, and he was right to do so, used to enjoy telling the story of how de Chirico, when painting his portrait before the war, had, through this gift of divination which is the special perquisite of poets, marked his forehead with a star at the point where a bullet was to strike him. In the same way Picasso's departure from Montparnasse was a warning from heaven. The war was nearly over. For Montparnasse died with the armistice.

There was never so much outlandish imagination, freedom and contradiction as during the war. The imagination in dress shown by the army, their tunics cut out of flowered upholstery velvet, will never equal the fantasy of Montparnasse. What made things complicated was that as a reaction to opium or homosexuality it was fashionable during the war to be bourgeois. And vice itself was practised in a bourgeois way. Married couples everywhere. If you didn't get married, you underwent conversion. Because for one generation youth had already come to an end. While knitting a muffler for her *poilu,* the Montparnasse wife would knit one for her lover, who was often waiting for peace to know what his nationality would be. At apéritif time, anyone dressed in the normal way needed more courage than a burglar climbing a wall topped with broken bottles before he could go through this hedge of mufflers, pullovers, scarves, multi-coloured hair, balaclavas, women with football boots, checked caps and made-up eyes. This inferno was as closely guarded as the garden of the Hesperides. All the more so because at each table were dogs, with whom their master shared the vermouth-and-blackcurrant, the bitters, dogs who like them drank more than they ate. Kisling's dog, Kousky-Kousky, wore a cloak, while the paintings in which the painter included him assured a life already miraculously long for a man, but even more so for a dog, while on the other hand you see eternal objects, such as a pipe, still-lifes that are stillborn, while so many unfortunate people went to La Rotonde and left behind them unfinished still-lifes, and although they were already dead it would have been inhuman not to finish them off. Miss U's bloodhounds, which had been as white as quickly seasoned clay pipes, and which should have been white, had turned the colour of Seltz water – when Libion the giant had his back turned, a kindly neighbour would pour torrents of Seltz water over them. In this human, inhuman bric-à-brac which included objects without value, but wearisome, you can imagine the price which could suddenly be attained by the cast of a statue by Monsieur Denys Puech. I'm looking for a man, Diogenes might have said. I was looking for a bourgeois. It didn't help Diogenes at all to say 'I'm looking for a man,' for a drunkard had mistaken his lantern for a place of ill-fame. At La Rotonde, in that human, inhuman bric-à-brac, I was looking for a bourgeois on whom to rest my eyes, just as, without looking for her, I might find a 'young lady'. Sitting among all those disguised women, I undressed them chastely with my eyes in order to transport them naked somewhere else and then dress them again. But you only find four-leaved clover by accident. But as you look you might pick a bunch of violets. In surprise, you drop the bunch. In that human, inhuman bric-à-brac, La Rotonde, I had to find a girl. At a dance-hall I'm sure no one would have noticed her but in this place it was her very insignificance that attracted attention. Anywhere else the modesty of her dress would have been only poverty. She stood up shortly after I had singled her out. I went to say good-day to one of the painters whom she was just leaving. He was muttering bad-temperedly: 'Odd sort of model who doesn't want to pose.' X. . . was an old-fashioned painter, and was treated as senile – He still believes in nudes, would say a cubist who boasted of having replaced *Le Journal* of the first still-lifes with *L'Intransigeant,* speaking of him with pity.

I questioned him. 'Here's a phenomenon for you. She puts on an act. Mademoiselle is so modest that she can't undress in front of one man, she has to have at least fifty of them. Let's say no more about it, anyway. And yet. . . .' I was embarrassed by her blush. And he began to relate a list of her charms in front of the poor girl who smiled stupidly in order to hide her embarrassment. 'What breasts, what buttocks! Just look at that fine flesh. You could eat those buttocks!' In this way he set out the poor girl's charms and she, obviously unaccustomed to anyone singing her praises, didn't know where to look. There was no need for him to tell me, I could see for myself. 'And yet,' X went on, 'I can't go to La Grande Chaumière like any schoolboy.'

'You're probably a painter,' she said to me.

I replied that I wasn't, but that I came here because I had friends. She seemed reassured. Shortly afterwards, as she got up, I got up too. I suggested going with her. She thanked me.

'You don't seem at home in these surroundings,' I told her casually. This remark doesn't mean anything, it flatters everyone.

'I'm glad you noticed it,' she replied with a sigh.

She was not one of those heroines from some novel, born to aspire to the highest reaches but losing everything. She had wanted to take advantage of her beauty in an honest way. No doubt, as everything doesn't fit into a simple pattern, people see two things a poor girl can do: either become a prostitute or do honest work, become a secretary-typist. She had not wanted to sit down in front of a typewriter or a sewing-machine. She was using her beauty honestly. Most of all she was lazy and as a little girl she used to spend whole hours in an armchair without moving, not doing anything, not reading. She hated fairy stories, and interrupted her maid whenever she wanted to tell her one. The only story she would tolerate was that of her early childhood, her misdeeds, the convulsions which overcame her whenever she was refused anything, the vases she pointed at with her little finger, and which her father had insisted once and for all be given to her, for fear she would go into one of those tantrums – all her impossible demands – then she would close her eyes, shuddering, and say with delight: 'How unbearable I was, in fact!'

She told me all this, adding: 'And I've no regrets. I broke those vases, but the Germans would have broken them anyway.'

This was how I learnt that she was a refugee. Her father and mother had been taken to a concentration camp. This proud girl had had all these humiliations. They had not affected her pride in any way.

I asked her as indirectly as possible, in order not to upset her, if the Germans had assaulted her in any way, but she said no; Prince Eitel had suggested he should marry her. Near Compiègne she had had a German soldier shot for trying to kiss her.

She lived alone in Paris, she had a two-room apartment in a furnished house near the Place de l'Etoile, her wall was decorated with a signed portrait of Prince Eitel. She lived in this early memory.

She was intoxicated, infatuated with herself, and this is what saved her. She wasn't upset by the fact that in the studio, although she was close to the stove, she felt herself getting colder, and through remaining motionless and becoming gradually icy in this way, she felt she was turning into a statue.

She left Colarossi for La Grande Chaumière.

She told me that the first day she posed at another Academy she was dismissed. For, not knowing the form, as one of the painters stood up and took hold of her foot in order to change its position slightly for she had moved – she had slapped his face and was sacked the same day. She did not mix with any of the models, who hated her.

I didn't see her again.

The next day I went to La Grande Chaumière. Although I had passed the age when a schoolboy trembles as he rings the doorbell of a brothel I felt some embarrassment, not so much at entering this place but rather the embarrassment you must feel in the army when you have to scrape carrots for the first time. I had never known how to hold a pencil. Lycée teachers are delighted when the duffers are absent from the drawing class. And when they attend they are sent to the back of the class and busy themselves behind their drawing-boards with things not wholly connected with drawing. But as I went in I was quickly reassured. I was late. My entrance was hardly noticed. I was not dealing with idlers. I obediently fixed a sheet of paper in place with four drawing-pins – and I looked at the model. It was a noble old man. 'Well now, he looks like God,' was my first thought. I didn't know how right I was. For I learnt afterwards that this peace-loving man had one defect – he thought he was God. . . . He posed without demanding any money and in the hope, once he had finished posing, that he could explain to all these budding painters: all religion, he would say, had been misrepresented.

Notebook II

The banks of the Marne, a nook where one can take one's rest for ever!

When I was a child Nogent seemed to me rather like a forbidden place – heaven or hell – how would I have known? It was just before the war – the period of the tango, and skating. Every Monday morning you could read in the papers about fights which had broken out the day before in one of those Nogent drinking places on the banks of the Marne. It was through the papers that I would learn of these shooting incidents, with revolver shots whose echo I would like to have overheard, with fewer ricochets along their path, shots which were fired over some suburban Helen. Avidly, I learnt that it needed only the intoxication of wine and love (one

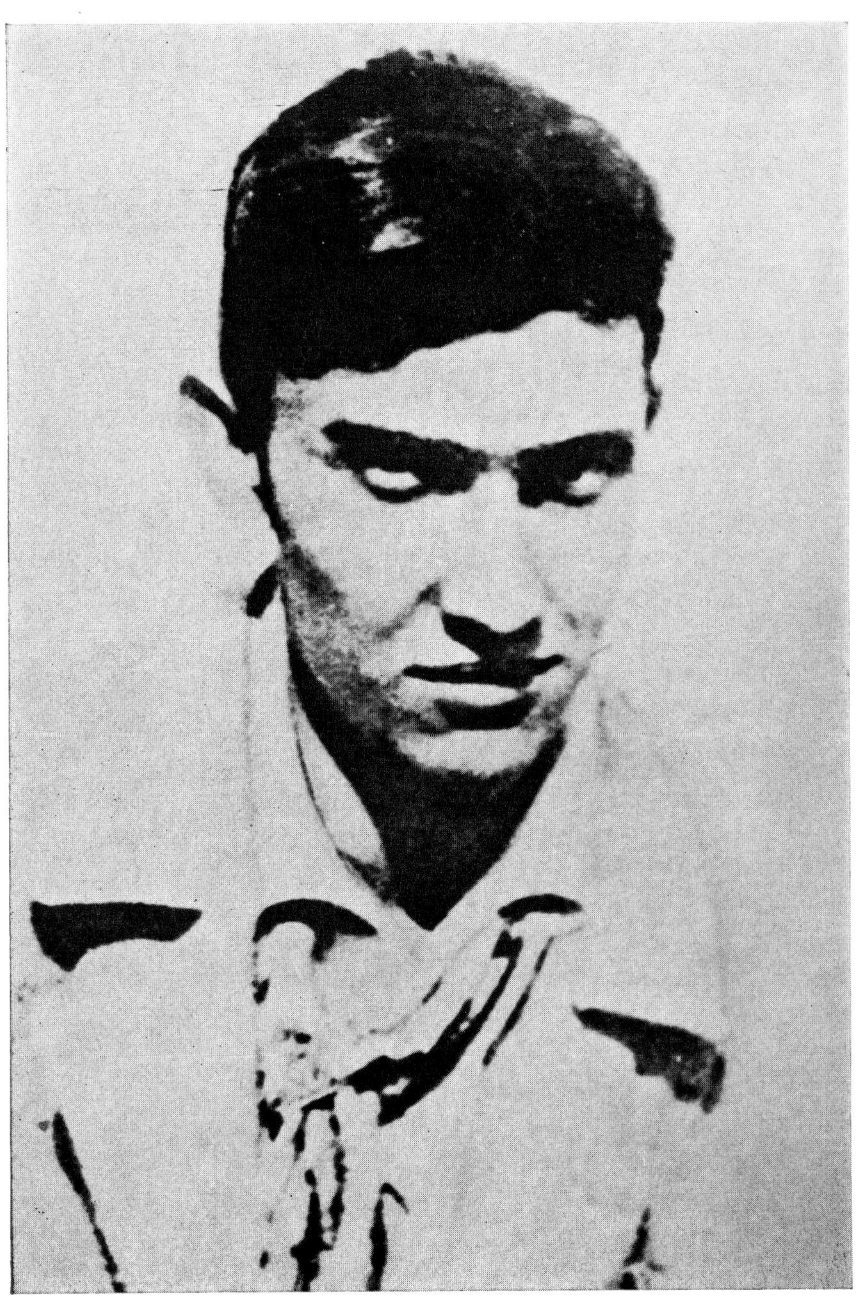

Raymond Radiguet.

Jean Cocteau as a young man. Drawing by Léon Bakst.

Above. Left to right: Jean Hugo and Jean Cocteau (standing), Pierre de Lacretelle and Radiguet (sitting). *Below.* Radiguet (centre) with Valentine and Jean Hugo at Magic City *c.* 1922.

Radiguet *c.* 1920 with his cane. Painting by Jacques-Emile Blanche.

never knows in what exact proportion they are blended) to awaken instincts so profoundly rooted within us that we cannot be aware of them.

But I was soon able to learn at the expense of my elders that life can be even cheaper and that all intoxication, even the most noble, is equally dangerous. In summer the Monday newspapers also set out the number of people drowned in accidents due to carelessness. I admired such carelessness.

I also remember the capture of Bonnot, at Nogent-sur-Marne. From a house protected with mattresses the criminal shot down everyone who moved forward. What a waste of heroism! But the Apaches who had escaped from Nogent would soon be able to give free rein to their warlike insticts, with nothing to fear beyond being taken for heroes.

Through what aberration, you will ask me, in astonishment, do you want to make Nogent, this place of ill-repute, as it appeared to you when you were very young, the setting for *fêtes galantes*? Why not? Love is not an innocent game and didn't those Apaches on the banks of the Marne restore its original ferocity?

But this Marne wasn't mine. And I hardly knew Nogent except through odd news items. When my brothers and I went for walks with my father nearly every Sunday we never went in this direction. It was usually a more tranquil Marne that we saw, towards La Varenne. We were living at Parc Saint-Maur. I was born there, I had never left it, and I was so much an animal in a 'park' that the word was correct in my case. I walked about there like a hind in a park, and I never sighed for a moment at thinking myself a prisoner. On the contrary I was proud of my native town, as though it had been my property, my domain. Everyone around me, except my father, was ignorant of its past and because of this ignorance it seemed to belong to me. I didn't imagine that any place on earth could be more noble than the one where I had been born. As I saw the Annamites from the Parangon boarding-school come out into the old street of Saint-Maur I would think of Madame de La Fayette who would go to take a rest there, in search of a little calm (Mme de La Fayette's phrase about Saint-Maur), not to dream there, for I don't see her as much of a dreamer, but to think at her ease, and, who knows? perhaps to write there one of those chronicles of the heart, those love stories about famous people, one of her historical novels. At Saint-Maur the names of the streets recalled this past to me: rue de Condé, avenue La Trémoïlle, avenue Médicis, and so many others! I was only to discover later the lines by Ronsard about the Château de Saint-Maur, the favourite residence of Catherine de Médicis. How I regret it, and if only they could have transported me there! On the other hand, on my way to school I often took the boulevard Rabelais, but this name did not speak to my heart. For it was not only famous names that I needed, and it meant nothing to me that the curé of Meudon might have been that of Saint-Maur. My brothers and I would often go and play on a mound that we would call 'the little mountain' by the banks of the Marne, where the Château de Condé had once stood. For our games of hide and seek we would even use, feeling frightened as we did so, an underground passage which was blocked up almost where it began, but it seemed to us endless and full of mystery, although it was mainly full of rubbish. With what redoubled attention did I read Piérard's (?) book on Saint-Maur – hoping to discover some new underground passage which I would be the only one to know – and how dramatic my games became when I associated them with the past.

I would contemplate, without understanding it, that audience, described by Sully, which Henri III granted to this future minister at the Château de Saint-Maur. Sully recounts that the king received him with a basket full of little dogs hanging round his neck and remained motionless, making no more movement than the idol on the Island of the Hermaphrodites! Nogent, a place of ill repute. . . .

But I certainly wasn't avid only for glory, and this pride in my birthplace was something I drew from myself rather than from Saint-Maur – for the banks of the Marne to which the only memories attached are not glorious but anonymous, those of the uninteresting couples who go for walks there, this youth which is continually renewed, like the water itself; what I cherished most was the Marne, without suspecting with what glory this river would soon cover itself.

A city childhood, whether rich or poor, seems to be deserving of pity. If a childhood is rich, how likely it is to be uninteresting! And for a sound heart, where envy cannot enter, how deep pleasures seem as soon as they are over and you are responsible for them! I would not exchange my memories for any others. That childhood as flat as a lawn, which for eleven years stretched as far as the eye can see on unbroken ground, how I like to roll on it now and delight in it. That rough grass where I thought I was running about in freedom . . . I remember the ground in the avenue des Rochers approaching our house from when I was very young. My memories! Like blades of grass they vary in height. Some higher than my head, others on the contrary are in danger of being trampled underfoot.

I can see myself when I was two, taken every morning by my nurse to the girls' school which my mother had left four years earlier. The gentle warmth of knees and breasts, I have never found it since, not as it was when I felt these caresses to be so different from those of my mother or my nurse. A different taste. . . .

And then I think that nothing develops sensuous pleasure so much as living among fruit. Remembering the cherries I picked from the tree is almost like the memory of a flirtation, and the apricots were as warm as a yielding body.

One place attracted me especially, and it seemed mysterious to me. It was the Ile d'Amour. During the Sunday walks with my father I had often seen on the river bank couples in light-coloured clothes ring a bell in order to summon the ferryman. As mysterious as an ancient ceremony – like the crossing of Charon. The ferryman was not paid. It must have been a pact with the devil.

One day, however, I was to go to the Ile d'Amour. We were coming back from Ormesson, dying of thirst, we were going to get something to drink there. I can still hear the sound of the barrel-games and the creaking of the swing. A couple were swinging on it. They were engaged and both of them lived quite near to our house.

Already the mere sight of the swing made too much impression on me and fired my imagination. The girl, her head thrown back, intoxicated with something, drunk (with swinging or with love), her head thrown back, her whole body offered, tense, with the irritating, obscene laughter of young girls (the indecent, nervous laughter which always seems to emanate from someone who is being tickled, so irritating that it makes you want to rape her, you don't know why, to satisfy yourself, or to stop them laughing, to gag them) would have represented fairly well in some allegory the monstrous indecency of virgins. Was her fiancé her lover? No matter. The swing creaked as though it was irritated too. *One person at a time on the swing*; a sign affixed to the gate. They seemed to go higher and higher. The fiancé, his knees braced, pushed harder and harder. The girl was clumsy and everything she did tended to cancel out the man's efforts. They went higher and higher. The laughter became more shrill, more irritable – all at once it turned into a cry. The swing was still up in the air, almost vertical to the supporting bar, but the young man was alone. Horrible image of love down on the ground, on the gravel, a girl in a white dress, lifeless, her breast open and bleeding, while the fiancé, carried up by the momentum, seeing her below, at his feet, unable to stop at once, was forced to wait until the swing slowed down before he could jump out. Ghastly seconds! One wonders what could be passing through this man's mind at such a moment. Sickened, I looked at the bleeding girl: ghastly spectacle which I see now as one of those savage ceremonies of antiquity, which would appear barbarous today, for the significance escapes us. Oh, that swing, the subject of an erotic print. It's no longer a question of looking at the white stockings or the place where the thighs are revealed. Not that at all. But on the ground in a pool of blood, a virgin dressed in white, and, on his knees beside her, a young man weeping. An image worthy of Greek tragedy. Of all the frivolous painting of the eighteenth century, Watteau's work is the only setting where a girl can fall out of a swing and die. This happened in June 1914. The scene moves me deeply; I feel there is still something pagan about it, a pagan grandeur. One person at a time on the swing. The couple had disobeyed the gods. During the first days of the war the fiancé wanted to join up. . . . He heads the list of the Saint-Maur dead fallen on the battlefield. Such conduct, such example, force you to think of fatality. And after such spectacles, and even more so, after the spectacle of the war, anyone in charge of people, a novelist, is well aware that he is not always free to find for his characters the dénouement that pleases him, that sounds right. In this way the death of a character who seems useless to us was often ordered in the same arbitrary fashion, yes, like fatality, especially for those who cannot sense the antique *fatum,* who do not know from the start of a novel that the hero must die.

Those who know the banks of the Marne understand the incomparably gentle nature of this river. Its waters seem more gentle than any others. Compare it for example to the river of which it is a tributary, the Seine; the Seine which is so dreary along all its course until it reaches Paris and seems to have been created only to cross this city, where it acquires its full value. But once it has crossed Paris it becomes sad again, a thin trickle. The Marne truly deserves to be immortalized by the heroism of an entire nation.

People remember perhaps the summer of 1914, although the events and the feelings they engendered turned us away from the spectacle of nature. That summer was particularly beautiful, and few months of August have been so prodigal with fruit, flowers and vegetables. But what poor compensation these gifts of Ceres were, alongside what the whole nation sacrificed to her: its best blood, the youngest, the freshest, flowed over her.

At Champigny, where all the military trains passed through the station, the strategic point of patriotism. Was it patriotism that I felt then? How can I know. But it is almost with gratitude that I think of the first days of the war, the sensations they brought me, the first upsets of war, admirable ones, I can only compare them to the first emotions of love that I was to feel three years later. But at the beginning of the war my physical being was shaken more deeply than at the beginning of love. If that is patriotism then I felt patriotic. All voices had a different sound. Things which would have seemed revolting awoke heroic thoughts. So much red wine spilt on the station platform; I thought of the virgin on the Ile d'Amour. But after a few days the military trains were no longer going in one direction only. The first wounded men passed through. Because of them the shouting was less loud, out of decency. Soon afterwards, all that has been inspired by decency having collapsed, the whole nation appeared more decent still.

Not a single boat now on the Marne. It looks as though they have all gone upstream, requisitioned by Charon.

Hills of France, you who please the eye like a woman's breasts, all these rash young men will roll on until they die. Ile de France with landscapes as gentle as our finest painting, charms like yours can make the heart forget its stricter duties. What a game for you then, on the contrary, to invite it there!

Fruit you gather yourself has a two-fold taste. This was how death offered itself, insiduously, to rash young people. . . . How attractive it was to pluck it from the branch. Is it ever possible again to reach it in advance, to pluck it before it is ripe?

Generous roads of Ile de France, fringed by apple trees, thus death, as round and perfect as fruit, offered itself to young people.

All these children no longer hampered by the presence of a maid, even a German maid, roll down the slopes of France as gentle as women's breasts, down to the end, down to death. All that blood spilt. I really think that the earth has never been so soft since the flood. Today we aspire to terra firma.

* * *

From the age of about seventeen Radiguet had been anxious to move ahead of the avant-garde, to write in an 'ordinary' way and link his admiration of the classics with the ideals he described himself as 'bourgeois'. Perhaps he was trying to express this feeling here in the first of the *Notebooks* when he described how Montparnasse at the end of the war was full of people who had set up house together. Being 'bohemian' had become dull, being 'bourgeois', at this stage at least, was advanced, even avant-garde.

The studiedly cynical start shows Radiguet trying hard to be more mature than he was, for he cannot have seen much of Montparnasse before 1918 and it was in any case too early to write its history. It is almost too early still, for in some ways Montparnasse has not yet come to an end. Possibly Radiguet intended these pages as the start of a novel or the story which he began at Le Lavandou and left unfinished. In the Club des Libraires edition of the *Oeuvres complètes* are some pages which appear to form its continuation, describing the narrator's failure to seduce the girl he had met in Montparnasse. Some French critics believe that the description of Montparnasse is a version of the one originally intended for the early part of his second novel, and then discarded as out of place.

Some of the names mentioned may seem obscure: Denys Puech was one of the best-known representatives of 'official' art. He lived from 1854 to 1942 and his respectable statues can be seen in the Luxembourg Gardens and other public places in Paris. Libion was the proprietor of La Rotonde, while Colarossi and La Grande Chaumière were the two big painting academies at the time.

The second *Notebook* is of particular value for what it tells us about Radiguet himself, and has been much quoted by his biographers. Intense and over-dramatized though these memories are, they sound more convincing than the over-coloured attempt to describe Montparnasse. The episode about the mad maid-servant in *Le Diable au corps,* which was based on fact, shows how impressionable Radiguet was as a child. The episode about the girl who was killed on the swing impressed him in the same way and led him to think about the relationship between love and death, a recurrent theme in Cocteau's later work. The Ile d'Amour is no name invented for the sake of symbolism – it is an island in the River Marne, close to Saint-Maur.

Radiguet's remarks about the beauty of France and the war he had seen as a boy sound sentimental today, but he was remembering the conversations he would have heard as he grew up, when patriotism, jingoism even, were normal feelings. At the beginning of *Le Diable au corps,* the narrator describes how his family would go every day after dinner 'to the station at J—, two kilometres away, to watch the troop trains go by'. France to Radiguet was in fact even more important for its literary history. He felt intense local patriotism for Saint-Maur and was especially delighted that the Château de Condé had been the country retreat of one of his favourite writers, Madame de La Fayette. In another prose piece entitled *Ile-de-France Ile d'Amour* he wrote that for him 'the feeling for *la patrie* is based entirely on literature'. French painting meant a good deal to him too, and even if the picture of the pink-clad girl on the swing is surely the famous painting by Fragonard, it is understandable that he attributes it to Watteau, whose work is more mysterious and full of foreboding. Just after the reference to this painting, Radiguet makes a point of stating that a novelist is not always free 'to find for his characters the dénouement that pleases him, that sounds right'. If his own novel had been finished when he wrote this, he may still have been pondering over the rightness of its conclusion.

During 1922 a few poems by Radiguet were published in magazines, but these were 'old' works, so to speak, for he was currently too preoccupied with prose to write verse. An extract from *Le Diable au corps* – the episode describing how the narrator coveted the Swedish girl Svéa – had appeared in *Les Feuilles libres* in February, although the book was not scheduled for publication for another year. Cocteau published two important books during this year. The first, *Le Secret professionnel,* owed a great deal to his discussions with Radiguet. Cocteau must surely have been thinking of his much-loved friend when he developed his theory about the 'angel' poets. He mentions Rimbaud and Verlaine, and also says that everything became clear to him when he discovered that in Hebrew the words 'angel' and 'angle' are synonymous. Later he was to write the moving poem *L'Ange Heurtebise,* in which the angel inhabits him. It has always been supposed that this was his way of taking Radiguet, who was dead by then, into his own entity. Many of the poems in *Vocabulaire,* his other major work published in 1922, were inspired by Radiguet and it looked as though Cocteau genuinely could not live without him.

Radiguet could no doubt have lived without Cocteau, emotionally at least. He seems to have written no poems to Cocteau, and even 'the most sealed of letters' that he wrote to Cocteau at the start of their relationship in 1919, ending with the declamation 'I adore you', provided him with striking phrases which he used without hesitation in one of his articles for *Le Coq*: 'Ever since 1789 they've been forcing me to think. It makes my head ache.' He did not write *to* Cocteau, but about him, well-reasoned articles full of suitable praise. Cocteau made many drawings of him during 1922 and 1923 and in all of them the young man is aloof, sometimes asleep, remote from Cocteau and the world in general. But during the summer at least there do not seem to have been any jealous scenes; many friends joined them but work went on almost without interruption.

Cocteau's letters to his mother describe how in July Radiguet had begun to write a new novel. Cocteau had expected to like it, but he had not anticipated the subject-matter. It was a far cry indeed from a sordid love-affair in the suburbs of Paris. This new novel was concerned with *le gratin,* the 'upper crust' of society, and according to Cocteau, who was wildly enthusiastic, was 'Finer than Proust and truer than Balzac'. No wonder Radiguet had been studying the *Almanach du Gotha,* the 'Who's Who' of the aristocracy. Cocteau was astonished to discover how much Radiguet had observed. Here were the results of his observations made while sitting in silence at Le Boeuf sur le Toit, at dinner parties, balls and other social occasions, watching and listening, while Cocteau and his friends talked and gossiped.

Cocteau had always defended Radiguet when his mother and various friends from his own milieu had attacked him. Now he discovered something else: Radiguet's family had an interesting ancestry. His mother was not only devoted to her children, but her family name had been Audifreddy, he wrote, therefore she was a 'Tascher, therefore a relative of Joséphine'. Like the Empress Joséphine, Madame Radiguet had been born in Martinique. 'This explains a whole Creole side of her son's character – why he sleeps during the day, smokes and likes sugar.' Madame Radiguet had actually been a Mademoiselle Tournier before her marriage. A little later Cocteau also discovered to his delight that his friend's father was probably descended from the Poisson-Pompadour family. The poem that resulted from these genealogical discoveries was hardly one of Cocteau's best and Radiguet must have found this particular form of flattery more than embarrassing. 'We should not be surprised,' wrote the poet, 'if your delicate strength adds the roses of love to the black laurel, for in you the blood of Joséphine is mingled with that of La Pompadour.' He evidently took all this more seriously than did the Radiguets themselves.

The group of friends left Le Lavandou when too many holiday-makers arrived there and moved to a villa at nearby Le Pramousquier. By the middle of August Radiguet had apparently written a hundred pages or so of his new book and Cocteau became even more enthusiastic, if that was possible, describing it as 'without doubt one of the finest novels in existence' and emphasizing the contrast with the previous book. The first had been a novel of *cynisme,* typical of extreme youth, whereas this was a novel of 'purity'. No sooner was it finished than editing and re-writing began. Radiguet had written several letters to Cocteau's mother while he was at work, thanking her for the kindness she had shown him – obviously their relationship was greatly improved – telling her about his own book and about her son's more varied compositions. He still related the rest of the world to literature. When he told her about a forest fire near Hyères he said that the entire landscape had a tragic beauty that 'only Chateaubriand could describe'. Jean still did not like Chateaubriand in spite of Radiguet's efforts to convert him, he told Madame Cocteau. He ought to read the *Voyage en Amérique,* which is 'the most astonishing thing in the world'. In another letter he said that he had read Marivaux's *Vie de Marianne* and been disappointed.

He also informed her that her son was now better (after a bad cold) and would return to Paris laden with plays, a novel and admirable poems. He himself had written only a novel but he had been able to concentrate with 'clairvoyance'. He said he would return too with 'some resolutions for the winter' and he felt he would keep them. He intended to visit his parents as soon as he was back to see his newly-born brother, the last of the Radiguet children. In a letter to Valentine Hugo he confessed that writing novels was much more entertaining than reading them.

Cocteau had in fact already told his mother about his work. He had done some drawings and an adaption of an Annamite play. He had been working 'passionately' at a novel, unconcerned about whether it would please other people or not. The main thing was that it pleased him, whereas poetry was suffering and criticism a game. He had discovered at last that it was essential to enjoy what one was writing and he was trying a mixture of the funny and the sad, the two sides of his nature.

Le Grand Ecart is indeed funny, and only sad perhaps because the hero, Jacques (i.e. Cocteau), is disturbed by the conflicting masculine and feminine sides of his nature. Having discovered that he too could write a novel, taking days rather than years over it, Cocteau went on to another. By the end of October he told his mother that he had not written earlier because he had been working day and night on a new book. He called it a short story but it was in fact longer than his novel. He was convinced he had achieved something important for himself and he was indeed right, for *Thomas l'Imposteur*, based on his experiences during the war, is one of the most striking and enduring of his works. This book seems to have taken him six days and one friend remembered later that his words about working day and night were literally accurate. He hardly left his work table and Radiguet brought his meals to him. He told his mother that 'Radiguet, who is a severe critic, thinks it is a success.' He admitted also that he had been modelling himself on Stendhal, just as Radiguet had chosen Madame de La Fayette as his model.

The distance between *Le Grand Ecart* and *Thomas* is as great – on a different level – as the distance between *Le Diable au corps* and *Le Bal du comte d'Orgel.* It has even been said that the character of Thomas, although based on that of Cocteau's friend Raoul de Castelnau, incorporated characteristics of Radiguet's, in particular his struggle to come to terms with reality. Radiguet himself found this problem relatively easy to resolve in books, difficult in life.

In the late autumn they returned to Paris, each with many pages of manuscript. Cocteau made few alterations to his, but Radiguet worked differently – it would take him nearly another year to finish his second novel. This summer holiday of 1922 had demonstrated once again how the two writers acted as powerful influences one upon the other. Cocteau claimed to have given Radiguet a hint for the ending of *Le Bal,* while the very fact that he himself turned to novel-writing with such enthusiasm shows clearly the influence of Radiguet on him and his work.

1923

Le Diable au corps, begun in 1919, edited and re-written amidst so much advice, criticism and coercion, eventually appeared in March 1923, after Bernard Grasset had prepared the way with a publicity campaign of a type and range hitherto unknown in France. He intensified the methods he had used to sell a recent edition of Hémon's *Maria Chapdelaine* – posters, bookshop displays, advance notices and reviews – and succeeded in taking literature into cinema newsreels, where he was photographed signing the contract with the young author. He made all possible capital out of Radiguet's youth: 'I did not say, "I have found a great novelist," ' Grasset wrote later, 'I simply said, "I have discovered a seventeen-year-old author".'

Radiguet, who was never modest, gave his publisher all possible support; the more photographs of himself he saw, the better he was pleased. The campaign was a success, in that all France knew about the book, but there was almost as much controversy about Grasset's campaign as about the novel itself. Many people felt that the campaign was overdone, and various writers and critics thought the book no better and no worse than many others. Files of yellowing press-cuttings faithfully preserved in the Grasset offices prove how much attention the book received. Many reviewers praised it but the more conservative were shocked by a story in which a schoolboy takes over a soldier's wife. It was denounced as an insult to French family life, a slight on the army. Radiguet, who enjoyed writing parody, was even parodied himself. One critic imagined a novel written by an authoress of eight, who announced that by eighteen she would of course be too old for literature.

Among Grasset's critics was Jean Cocteau. Perhaps he had

hoped to run the campaign himself, and felt a little jealous. In a lecture he accused Grasset of replacing the 'curse of silence' with the 'curse of noise', adding that it was he, Grasset, who had *le diable au corps.* The campaign, in his opinion, had overwhelmed the book, it had to struggle for its existence, but at least this meant the book had to live through its own merit. Cocteau's lecture was later delivered to an audience of students, and apparently on this occasion Radiguet himself was present.

Le Diable au corps was, needless to say, a runaway best-seller. Radiguet distributed many signed copies and received some illuminating letters of thanks. Max Jacob hoped that for his taste the next book would be 'less cruel and more chaste'. Paul Valéry, impressed by its clarity, directness and 'closed' quality, hoped Radiguet would keep his independence and freedom of mind. Roland Dorgelès, who had written about the war from a soldier's viewpoint in his famous novel *Les Croix de bois,* was shocked that a young man could be so heartless, and told him so.

Dorgelès later became involved in a confused story which added to the novel a real-life sequel comparable only to a novelette. Radiguet had announced that his book was not autobiographical, but not everyone believed him. Then, so the story goes – and there is no proof that it is true – Alice appeared again in Paris. She was not upset by the book and did not object to having been 'killed off'. She came to Le Boeuf sur le Toit in the hope of finding Radiguet, because she had once lent him fifty francs and thought that now she had a chance of getting it back. She may have come with other intentions, but since Radiguet wasn't there she was forced to deal with Cocteau instead. Another story, which is fully documented in Robert Baldick's introduction to his translation of *Le Diable au corps,* is that Alice's husband, Gaston, visited Dorgelès in 1952 and complained that the book had ruined his life. Gaston died in 1954, leaving Dorgelès a statement in which he accused Radiguet of stealing his wife's diary, and a copy of *Le Diable* annotated with pathetic comments in which he tried to prove his wife's innocence. For example, where Radiguet had written that Marthe hands her lover a pair of her husband's pyjamas, Gaston had commented: 'I had no pyjamas.'

The issue that obsessed him, and of course has fascinated journalists ever since, was whether Radiguet was the father of Alice's son. Alice died in 1952, having always told her husband that their son was his own, and the son himself had stated that he was perfectly happy with the parents who brought him up. Baldick, however, mentions that the boy was left with a nurse for his first five years and that Gaston admitted to Dorgelès: 'I behaved badly towards the child. I kept him away from the time he was born.'

The truth will obviously never be known, and it is not a matter of any great interest or importance. Probably Cocteau was right when he remarked: 'If Radiguet had had a son he would have been proud of the fact and would have told everyone.' And according to Jean Desbordes, Cocteau's friend in the 'thirties, Gaston made an appointment with Radiguet shortly after the publication of the book. Cocteau and other friends were close at hand in case of trouble. When Gaston arrived, so *this* story goes, he told Radiguet that he had been 'overwhelmed by the book and was proud to appear in it'. It was Cocteau's belief and again one must point out that he obviously did not want to believe that *Le Diable au corps* was the literal truth – that Gaston tried as hard as he could to identify himself with 'Jacques' in the novel, and that he wanted to draw attention to himself.

If it should be suggested again, as it was at the time and has often been since, that boys of sixteen do not have experiences of this sort with older women, the newspapers, which Radiguet so enjoyed reading, prove that they do, often with tragic results. In 1968 a French teacher of thirty, Gabrielle Russier, had a love affair with one of her pupils, Christian Rossi, who was sixteen at the time. She was dismissed from her post, found guilty of *détournement de mineur* (corruption of a minor) and sent to prison. There she killed herself. In other circumstances her story could have been that of Marthe.

The title, *Le Diable au corps,* it should be remembered, does not produce any particularly dramatic effect in France; whereas its literal translation into English produces something of a shock on first encounter. To have *le diable au corps* is a colloquial phrase, obviously based on the medieval concept of possession by the devil, but meaning merely 'full of devilment', or, as the dictionary puts it, 'to be a tireless dancer'. Molière uses the phrase on several occasions. Possession? The narrator of Radiguet's novel *is* possessed, but by his feelings for Marthe, by a wish to dominate, by sexual infatuation, by a latent cruelty, and by jealousy.

Some critics in fact commented on the narrator's 'latent cruelty', without perhaps realizing that the average adolescent *is* cruel, for he still possesses his schoolboy destructiveness and has not yet learnt how to love. One critic, André Germain, decided that Radiguet had written two hundred pages, using a story which occupied two lines, without losing the reader's interest for a moment. He also added that nothing so immoral had been written since Laclos's *Les Liaisons dangereuses* in the eighteenth century. Radiguet would have been pleased at such a comparison; *Les Liaisons dangereuses* was one of his favourites. Germain also mentions something which is still intriguing today: the author's 'coquettish', fascinated pleasure in his own analyses – 'The cerebral pleasure is stronger than the carnal pleasure and this Cherubino of 1917 finds less satisfaction in his raptures than in his awareness of their unnatural quality.' Perhaps the devil was at work after all.

Radiguet was more or less satisfied with the attention he received. He told his father in a letter later that year that he had been taken by surprise when he read in a review full of praise a denunciation of his hero as 'the future capitalist, the factory manager who will cheat his workers just as he lied to Marthe.' He found this comment very strange, but remarked, a little cynically, that it would be a good sign if there were more silly remarks like this: it was a sign that the book was destined to become a classic, that more and more readers would find in it overtones relevant to situations far beyond a love affair in Saint-Maur. The review was in *Le Libertaire*, and reflected the editorial stance of the paper; but Radiguet was right, even today the reader finds unexpected identifications throughout the book.

Radiguet was also given a chance to comment on Grasset's controversial campaign, and on the vexed question of his age, or lack of age. On publication day an article entitled *'Mon Premier Roman'* appeared in *Les Nouvelles littéraires.* In it Radiguet said that, as the author, he might perhaps have objected to all this excitement about a novel which few people had had the chance to read. But he did not feel like that; he wanted to express not only his personal gratitude but that of his whole generation for they had benefited from facilities unknown to their elders. If he had been presented as a child prodigy, it was because people wanted to see things that way. '. . . One must live before one can write. But I would like to know at what stage one has the right to say: "I have lived." '

Radiguet spent most of his time with men and women older than himself, and always wished he was older, but he was nevertheless intensely aware of his own generation in the post-war world. Was it surprising, he asked in his article, if a book about adolescence should not express that 'anxiety' which had become so fashionable lately? 'But for the hero of *Le Diable au corps* (who in spite of the use of "I" should not be confused with the author), his tragedy lies elsewhere. This tragedy is due more to circumstances than to the hero himself. Freedom and idleness caused by the war influence a boy and kill a young woman.' He went to some lengths to point out that the 'little love story' was not a confession, even if it appeared to be one, and that the false autobiography is precisely the one that seems most true.

Le Diable au corps made him rich. His experiences, his fantasies, Alice and Gaston, they were all in the past now, he had used them and had become a successful writer, his ambition since the age of fifteen. Now that he had money he was free to live away from home and away from the anonymous, sometimes sordid hotels in which he stayed in Paris and in which he had started both his serious writing and his emotional life with Cocteau. He chose a place that many young men would have found dull and formal, but it was part of his nature to break the rules of the literary and artistic worlds. He took a room at the Hôtel Foyot in the rue de Tournon, near the Luxembourg Gardens; the hotel was a favourite of the members of the Senate which met nearby. Radiguet's brother René went there with him sometimes and remembers it as 'austere'. The manageress was proud of her new guest and of her signed copy of *Le Diable au corps.* The hotel had a good, slightly old-fashioned restaurant and the young celebrity would eat there. At least one of his restaurant bills has been preserved, and if it is typical it shows that he either possessed a large appetite or was making up for his years of comparative poverty. On this occasion he began with a fillet of sole *dieppoise,* followed it with fried sole, pheasant *carême,* cheese, an ice and a meringue, ending with coffee and a liqueur. To help it down he drank a cocktail, a bottle of champagne *nature* and a bottle of Chambertin 1898 at 50 francs. Even if he was entertaining a guest, it was a not inconsiderable meal.

His happy attachment to material pleasures may have prevented him from being upset by an incident related to the non-material world. During the spring of 1923 a few spiritualist sessions were held at the Hugos' apartment in Paris. Radiguet and Cocteau seem to have been present at each one, Paul Morand and Georges Auric occasionally. A 'spirit' spoke to the group through a small table – it was black, with painted flowers – and although the spirit 'said' various obscure things about several other people, it was very direct when asked about Radiguet:

'Talk to us about Radiguet again.'

'Uneasiness will grow with genius.'

'What uneasiness?'

'Uncertainty.'

The spirit made references to Martinique, where Radiguet's mother had been born, and when Cocteau asked it to give its name it replied: 'Beauharnais'. Asked again to say something interesting, it replied: 'He should love me for he loves nothing.' The following week the spirit was again asked who it was. 'I am death,' came the reply. The friends then decided to end these disturbing seances.

The spirit had, however, made one mistake. It had said that Radiguet would not win the prize. This was the Prix du Nouveau Monde, for which the money came from the United States through the endeavours of Bernard Fay, who had already helped Radiguet two years earlier. An American lady, well-read in French literature, presented the prize money as a token of her admiration for France and to foster the friendship she hoped would always exist between the two countries. The prize was to be awarded to a recently published novel which deserved the attention of the public in both countries. In order to select it Bernard Fay needed a jury of seven. He approached Cocteau, who knew the young French writers so well; Fay wanted a young jury. The other members were the cosmopolitan Paul Morand, Jean Giraudoux, who was well known in the United States, Valéry Larbaud, gifted and popular, Jacques de Lacretelle, whose reputation was growing, and the complicated Max Jacob, who in fact delegated his vote to Cocteau.

Fay was inundated with manuscripts and found to his horror that they were all imitative, the most popular models being Paul Bourget, André Gide and the popular, unliterary Maurice Dekobra, while passages in imitation of Lautréamont were occasionally added in the hope of causing a sensation. The unfortunate Fay was bribed with gifts and the interminable reading gave him mental indigestion and kept him awake at night. Cocteau had no intention of struggling through all the books. After the luncheon party – French literary prizes are usually decided over lunch – Cocteau 'went onto the attack and threw the name of Radiguet at us like a burning hand grenade'. The possible immorality or amorality of *Le Diable au corps* were discussed, but the jury decided that they were not influenced by considerations of this sort. There was in fact only one serious rival, Philippe Soupault, best known as a surrealist poet, who had written a literary *roman à clef, Le bon Apôtre,* about the clashes between Apollinaire's rivals after his death. Paul Morand, although a friend of Radiguet and Cocteau, voted for Soupault; so did Giraudoux and Larbaud. Fay himself, and Cocteau, obviously, voted for Radiguet; Jacob's vote went with Cocteau's. A vote from Jacques de Lacretelle made *Le Diable au corps* the winner. The nervous Max had not even read the novel in its entirely and worried that the parts he had *not* read might have been 'anti-religious and obscene'. The patron in Washington found the book 'interesting', but said with apparent politeness that it wasn't quite what she had been looking for. Nor did it please the American Legion, who objected on much the same grounds as Dorgelès. The American press, however, gave the book wide coverage, but it did not reach a large public there, especially as no English translation was available until 1932.

Radiguet could now enjoy himself; he had both fame and

money. Probably the most attractive aspect of his character was his devotion to his family, and now, his father being ill, he more or less supported them. Cocteau admired him for this, especially since Radiguet did not mention it and his friend only discovered his generosity by accident. He was, in fact, trying to loosen Cocteau's hold on him. He remarked unkindly that he did not want to be known at the age of forty as 'Madame Cocteau'. Women found him more attractive than ever, and he was still drawn to foreigners – notably the attractive young Bronja Perlmutter, a Polish girl whom he may have met through the painter Kisling, or may, according to some friends, have picked up, together with her sister, at a dance-hall. Radiguet even talked of marrying her, but again, according to friends, this was part of his anti-Cocteau campaign.

Nevertheless, he continued to see Cocteau regularly, and even went to England with him in April 1923. They visited Oxford, which Radiguet described to Valentine Hugo as a 'paradise without eves'. He found it an 'admirable city' and 'like its poets'. He had time to notice the 'deer, architecture both Gothic and Greek, lawns "enamelled" with pre-Raphaelite flowers'. Cocteau preferred the shops, and according to Francis Steegmuller, both men were fascinated by striped knitted gloves, buying several pairs for themselves and their friends. It was a cold spring that year and after a visit to Cocteau's friend Reginald Bridgeman, former secretary to Lord Derby in Paris and now living in Harrow, they were glad to return to France.

In May he accompanied Cocteau when the latter was delivering his lecture *Order Considered as Anarchy* at the Collège de France. Cocteau said a good deal about Radiguet and his book: he believed it was the answer to 'accursed' literature – it appealed to him, and it appealed to typists. Cocteau mentioned Max Jacob, Paul Morand and other friends, but Radiguet was the star of his show: 'With *Le Diable au corps,*' he said, 'I considered I had backed a winner.'

A second novel, after his first success, is a problem for any writer. This hard task now lay ahead of Radiguet. Although many people who met him found him 'old' and disillusioned, he was barely adult. Another hurdle lay before him: the compulsory call-up into the French army. He had to edit and revise the book he had written the previous year and hardly touched since, although he and Cocteau had read sections to friends. The two friends set off again for Le Picquey, intent on hard work. In a letter to his father Radiguet explained that there was a vast amount of re-writing to be done and that the book would be very long. He also asked him to send candles, so that he could work at night, there being no electricity.

If *Le Diable* had been completed with difficulty, *Le Bal* was a distillation from a vast amount of material, much of it jettisoned in the end, a novel pared down to the strictest minimum. Radiguet worked long and hard.

The resemblances in the novel's plot to Madame de La Fayette's best work, *La Princesse de Clèves,* are obvious. The hero, François, devoted to Anne, the Comte d'Orgel, realizes he is in love with the Comte's wife. He remains silent, but she becomes aware that they love each other. What can they do? Nobly she makes it clear that her duty is to stay with her husband, who has discovered her feelings. He knows how she will behave. The two men remain friends and honour prevails.

There will always be controversy about this novel. Is it static, negative, imitative? Does it show the author's uncertainty about his sexual direction; why else would he give the count a woman's name (in fact, by no means unusual in France) and choose the unfeminine 'Mahaut' for the heroine? Perhaps more pertinent is the criticism that the aphoristic judgements which sound so convincing seem to come from outside the characters, not from within as they did in *Le Diable.* Every sentence is absorbing, but the author seems to be writing from a great distance in time and space. The formality of the characters' behaviour is echoed in the punctilious style, full of inversions and imperfect subjunctives, always correct, but somehow too correct. Everything about *Le Diable* had been young, too much about *Le Bal* is old; it is only fair to add, however, that Radiguet's editing was probably not the final editing – that, as will be seen later, fell into the hands of others.

Why did Radiguet choose to write about a social class he knew only through Cocteau and his friends? He did so partly because he was consciously applying the techniques of the classical writers –

characters unconcerned with the problems of everyday life could devote their time to personal relationships and give the author every chance to analyse their development, point at morals and draw conclusions. Radiguet has been accused of social climbing, of being anxious to be accepted by the families whose invitations had reached him through Cocteau. He had certainly enjoyed the fancy-dress balls so popular at the time. Hostesses vied with each other in choosing themes, but few people outdid the annual ball given by the Comte Etienne de Beaumont, who in 1922 required each guest to come dressed as a game, while the following year they were to be characters from the age of Louis XIV. For the first ball Radiguet had appeared as a fairground shooting gallery, for the second he joined the retinue of a countess who represented an 'imaginary invalid', named after Molière's play. He painted spots on his face and looked as though he had measles.

Radiguet enjoyed these occasions, and it is well known that the 'ball' in the novel was based on the Comte de Beaumont's entertainment. But nobody reading *Le Bal du comte d'Orgel* could really think that Radiguet accepted this world as a comfortable place where everyone behaved with dignified and intelligent charm. In two of the novel's most important scenes he dismisses them, subtly, as selfish and, with rare exceptions, unthinking. In presenting his characters he reveals unexpected skill in dealing with a group of people involved in social confrontation. For example, the hero is on his way with the Comte d'Orgel and his party to a dancing-place at Robinson, just outside Paris. (It was indeed a well-known haunt for this set for two decades.) At the Porte d'Orléans, on the way out of the city, the Comte's car is halted. He sees his friend the Princesse d'Austerlitz, in full evening dress, directing her chauffeur's efforts to repair *her* car. The Princesse belongs not to the true aristocracy but to the nobility created orginally by Bonaparte, the *noblesse d'Empire*. The Comte is friendly with her, thereby proving that he is not a snob. On this occasion there is no shortage of idle spectators, *'la révolution inoffensive'*, who had acquired the habit of gazing at the well-dressed aristocracy at the *barrières*: splendid entertainment, free of charge. The Princesse, because of her origins, knows how to talk to the crowd, but suddenly one man is heard saying, 'If only I had some hand grenades!' A guest in the d'Orgel party is alarmed. But the Princesse asks the subversive man to help her, which he does. She then offers him wine and they drink togther. Radiguet adds one comment: 'This is how *coups d'état* happen.' If he had lived, would he have seen the world through the eyes of a social psychologist?

When the Comte and his party are preparing for the ball which gives the novel its title, Anne d'Orgel, as a joke, puts on a Tyrolean hat belonging to his guest, the exiled Russian Prince Naroumof. The Prince does not care for the gesture as the hat had been given to him by Austrian friends 'who couldn't offer me anything else'. The Prince has already been forced to tell fellow guests that not all revolutionaries can be condemned out of hand. Radiguet skilfully combines the Prince's reaction with that of Mahaut d'Orgel. Suddenly she has seen an opportunity for studied 'bad' behaviour, an opportunity to discourage François, who is deeply in love with her. With an uncharacteristically crude gesture she puts on the hat herself. Only the perceptive Naroumof almost guesses the reasons for her behaviour. He has learnt from suffering, and he is Russian: 'two reasons,' adds the author, 'which allowed him to have better understanding of the *bizarreries du coeur.*'

Possibly Colette remembered this scene when she wrote *The Képi,* a story in which the heroine puts on a man's képi as a joke. Her action reveals something of her true nature to the hero, who realizes he no longer loves her. Colette's subtlety here is different from Radiguet's, and she is dealing with only two people, whereas Radiguet is dealing with four, a husband and wife, the wife's would-be lover, and an outsider. The scene in *Le Bal* is a measure of his skill and it is worthwhile remembering a note he wrote about his own book: ' "Society" side: Atmosphere useful for the development of certain feelings, but it's not a picture of society; different from Proust. The décor doesn't count.' But perhaps it counted more than he knew, if only because he was looking at it from the outside. Of the style he said it was 'badly written', just as elegance must look as though it is badly dressed.

There is nothing 'badly written' about another scene; indeed it is remarkable for its moral suspense. The hero, François, is made to suffer because he has told a lie. He has said that his mother is away because he does not wish an invitation to be offered to her. Instead he wants to see Mahaut d'Orgel, whom he loves with such desperation, 'against the background of his childhood', by the River Marne. But as the party is lunching at a restaurant François's mother drives by in her carriage, and François hears it. Only Mahaut sees her, but pretends not to. François does not turn round. Radiguet describes the scene as an unmoved observer:

'The victoria passed. He closed his eyes, like a drowning man.

'Never had Madame de Séryeuse looked so young. Mahaut knew her only in dark-coloured gowns. Her country-style dress, straw hat and sunshade made her look like a younger sister to François.

'At the apparition Mahaut thought she was dreaming. She uttered a cry. The victoria had vanished.'

Like other rapidly-passing moments in Radiguet's work, the scene almost demands the film camera. (*Le Bal* was in fact filmed by Marc Allégret in 1969, adaptation and dialogue by Françoise Sagan.)

The author had written the note about 'décor' at Le Picquey as he remodelled his book, sacrificing many scenes, some of which have since been published in France. They are all interesting in themselves, especially the description of a journey from Paris to the suburbs on the last train which took people home after the theatre. Amusing though it is, the scene would have been out of place in the novel as we have it. And if Radiguet had kept the Negro servant Marie, whom he had originally introduced as a character in her own right, then he would have written the 'long novel' he mentioned to his father, with many more references to life in Martinique. What he achieved cost him a great deal of work, in which he had help of various kinds. Georges Auric had a typewriter and Radiguet dictated to him. Cocteau said later that in the afternoons he helped Radiguet to tidy up his book, and the amount of this help has long been a matter for speculation. It is true that the manuscripts show many remarks and suggestions by Cocteau but no actual amendments, and Auric has stated definitely that Radiguet *did* write his own book.

If Alice and Gaston had reacted to *Le Diable au corps* in different ways after publication, there had already been reaction to *Le Bal* before it was finished. When Cocteau and Radiguet had read parts of it to friends in Paris there had been plenty of enthusiasm even if the Comtesse Edith de Beaumont had fallen asleep. Anne d'Orgel was known to be a caricature of her husband, and Mahaut (Radiguet borrowed the name from Madame de Chabannes) has been regarded as a composite portrait, embodying some traits of the author's mother. Jean Hugo has in fact established a detailed 'key' for the characters in the novel, and few of them were totally imaginary. Naroumof was based on Prince Volkonsky, Mirza on Prince Firouz of Persia. The Princesse d'Austerlitz was known to be Princesse Murat, Madame de Séryeuse was said to be Madame Cocteau, while Paul Robin was a combination of Georges Auric and Paul Morand. Radiguet used people, places, names that he knew, even the name of a fisherman he had often listened to in Le Lavandou. His friends became intrigued by the game of identification and Valentine Hugo seriously but mistakenly thought at one moment that she was Mahaut d'Orgel.

Cocteau was anxious for the book to be published. He himself had done only a little revision to his two novels, and *Thomas* was published in October, while the friends were still at Le Picquey. It had been a curious holiday, with rain at the beginning and cold at the end. There was some sunshine though, and some adventures. Radiguet is said to have narrowly escaped drowning when he swam out too far from the shore. He ate a great many oysters, often in the company of Valentine Hugo who enjoyed them as much as he did. He may even have found time to write, in collaboration with Cocteau, the story called *La Ville au lac d'argent,* a romantic tale about a girl who becomes a prostitute, falls in love and returns to the purity of adolescence. The manuscript is in Radiguet's handwriting, scrawled so quickly as to be almost illegible. He and Cocteau would sometimes have competitions in the evenings to see who could devise and write a story most quickly. *La Ville au lac d'argent* has no particular quality except a kind of melancholy fluidity and occasional statements that associate it with Radiguet; for instance the heroine, when she was eighteen, wanted to be thirty. Then – and this sounds more like Cocteau – at twenty she wanted to be fifteen.

More important was Radiguet's decision to tidy up all his papers and manuscripts and persuade his brother René – to whom he offered money as a reward – to send him the proofs and original manuscript of a book of poems, which he thought could be found in his former bedroom. 'A disorganized man who is going to die and doesn't suspect it suddenly becomes orderly. His life changes. He sorts his papers. He rises early, he goes to bed early. He gives up his vices. His entourage congratulate him. In this way his sudden death seems all the more unfair. *He was going to live a happy life.*' Radiguet himself wrote these lines, but not at Le Picquey in 1923. They occur near the end of *Le Diable au corps* and have been quoted many times, by Cocteau and others, for it is so easy to develop hindsight. To be realistic, Radiguet sorted his papers because his mind so teemed with ideas he had to jettison some of them. He was seriously interested in a book about the early poet Charles d' Orléans and collected information about him. Cocteau said that Radiguet was fascinated by his debts, not only his poetry. There were other notes about other books, memories, plans, all of them found after his death in a dossier labelled 'Disorder', as though he did not know what to do with them.

One of the most interesting documents was entitled 'draft for a preface to a collection of poems', and it differs greatly from the preface published in the revised collection of *Les Joues en feu* in 1925. In the draft he is hesitant and had obviously changed his mind about some of his work. He had decided, he said, to suppress his poems in regular metre because their air of perfection, which he knew to be false, made them less interesting. But there was more hesitation to come, for the final edition included these poems, and the final preface refers to them, saying that they are all in regular metre because they were composed all at the same time in 1921, by the Mediterranean. And in certain of them 'the most greedy sensuality conceals itself least.'

Greedy sensuality during this holiday seems to have been limited to oyster-eating and the odd bout of secret drinking. Radiguet would talk endlessly to the attractive and musical Bolette Natanson, encouraging her to tell him all she could about the workings of a woman's mind. A note among his papers seems to show that Bronja Perlmutter wrote to him occasionally. The achievement of the holiday was the revision of his novel and although later his friends were quick to see curious premonitions of death during the summer Radiguet himself was probably more preoccupied with the mundane question of his military service, which by now had been put off simply until the proofs of his new novel were ready for correction.

In September Jean and Valentine Hugo left Le Picquey for their house at Fourques, going by way of Bordeaux. Valentine was not feeling well. However, the four of them had a good lunch in the town and Radiguet and Cocteau returned to their village the next day. Autumn was coming and soon they were back in Paris.

Radiguet went to the Hôtel Foyot and Bronja joined him. There was still work to do on *Le Bal,* and as usual the atmosphere of Paris did not encourage him to do it. He tried, but his 'disorder' had not all been put away in that file at Le Picquey and it overtook him again. In addition he did not feel well, he felt stomach pains and was occasionally seized with fits of shivering. He refused to take medical advice and although Bronja Perlmutter looked after him devotedly he became steadily worse. Cocteau had also heard from the south that Valentine Hugo was no better. Eventually Radiguet was seen by Cocteau's physician, Docteur Capmas, who had a great reputation but had already failed to save Apollinaire. He could not help Radiguet. In early December another doctor diagnosed typhoid fever and he was sent to a private nursing home in the rue Piccini. He had probably eaten some bad oysters. News came from the Hugos that Valentine had typhoid too. She was threatened by peritonitis but recovered after an operation in Montpellier on 11 December.

Alcohol and chaotic living had caught up with Radiguet even more than oyster-eating. He had no resistance left. In a strange way perhaps he no longer wanted to live, feeling himself imprisoned within his relationship with Cocteau. By relying on an unreliable doctor Cocteau had hardly helped him. Now he came to see him in the nursing home, but was accused by Gabrielle Chanel of being frightened of typhoid. Radiguet's mother visited him and did indeed catch the disease. Madame Cocteau sent Radiguet medallions of Notre Dame des Victoires. Cocteau chronicled the last few days and wrote Radiguet's words into theatrical dialogue:

'Listen,' he told him on 9 December, 'listen to a terrible thing. In three days I shall be shot by the soldiers of God.' Cocteau tried to argue. 'Your information,' Radiguet went on, 'is not so good as mine. The order has been given. I heard the order.'

A little later he said: 'There is a colour moving about and people are hidden in this colour.' Cocteau could not drive them away, he said, for he could not see the colour. Later still, he was able to tell his father how much he loved him.

In spite of his loving family and all his friends in Paris Radiguet died alone in the early hours of 12 December, his face contorted with pain. It relaxed later, perhaps, said some of his friends, because a priest had come.

Cocteau collapsed when he heard the news but could not bring himself to see Radiguet in death, as he had seen Proust. Darius Milhaud, in a letter to Francis Poulenc, said that it was perhaps better that way, better that he did not see 'that tragic swollen face with the half-open mouth and the head thrown back'. Cocteau contented himself with writing a dramatized account of this death in *Le Livre blanc* five years later.

He did not go to the funeral. Gabrielle Chanel, and Misia Sert, who had figured in *Thomas l'Imposteur,* paid the expenses of a mass at the church of Saint-Honoré d'Eylau and burial at Père Lachaise cemetery. 'It was most wonderfully done,' Nina Hamnett recalled. The weather was foggy and wet, the church was full of white flowers and famous people, Picasso, Brancusi, the composers Radiguet had known and the Negro band from Le Boeuf sur le Toit. Cocteau was too ill to come. Everything was white, even the coffin, for Radiguet, *homme de lettres,* as the cards of notification had said, was not yet twenty-one. Nina Hamnett and Marie Beerbohm and everyone else wept. 'It was the most tragic sight that I have ever seen,' wrote Nina Hamnett, 'Radiguet's sisters, the youngest being about six, stood in a row, their faces contorted with weeping. Marie and I burst into tears and went out into the street to see the procession start off. The hearse was covered in white and was drawn by two large white horses, like those in the war picture by Uccello in the National Gallery. They stood patiently and waited. The coffin was carried out with its white pall, and on it was one bunch of red roses. Many wreaths were carried out, and by the time the procession started the white hearse and a carriage following it were covered with white flowers. We walked down the boulevard, following the procession, and waited and watched the hearse and the long train of mourners disappear into the distance on their way to Père Lachaise. It was not yet ten o'clock and still pouring with rain.' The two women went into a café and drank brandy.

Milhaud wrote to Poulenc that he would tell him 'many painful and sad things about these mournful days. There were quite a lot of people and friends at the funeral, at the church (it's so easy to sign a register to indicate one's presence) but very few went as far as Père Lachaise. It was heartbreaking out there.'

Radiguet did not die with his death. His new novel, his poems, letters, the unfinished work, all eventually appeared. He has been much translated, filmed at least once and studied in many contexts. He did not die, neither did Cocteau, although many thought he would. He was referred to in Paris as *'le veuf sur le toit'*, the widower on the roof. He took to opium, but mainly he took to work, as he had always done, and his irrepressible creativity carried him along. He made new friends and found new lovers, but none of them replaced Radiguet for none of them had his talent and all the rewarding complexity that it entailed. Radiguet had been pleased to accept Cocteau's help with much of his work, and with *Le Bal* during the months before he died. Had he lived, he would probably have moved further away from Cocteau, but his death enabled the older man to keep him close, closer perhaps that he had ever been during their life together.

It was obviously Cocteau who prefaced *Le Bal* when it appeared the following year. He was hurt when some influential critics received it coolly. Jacques Rivière, for example, believed that it showed 'no sign that [Radiguet] would take his place among the great explorers of the human heart'. He believed Radiguet to be a writer of great sensitivity and promise, trying to overcome his weakness by studying the masters of the past. 'In psychology,' he added, 'I shall always give the advantage to discovery.' Cocteau did not forgive him. Other critics were quick to point out that Cocteau must have 'improved' the book and recent research has in fact found much mystery in the relationship between the typed text (with some handwritten amendments by Radiguet), the original edition as approved by Radiguet, and the definitive edition, revised by Jean Cocteau and Joseph Kessel. The latter wrote after Radiguet's death that the author had taken the proofs to the clinic with him. Thirty years later he said that Radiguet had not seen them. The reading public, however, has accepted the novel in the form that Grasset published it, with its breathtaking moments of stylistic finesse, but marred, perhaps, for present-day readers by the frequent use of the imperfect subjunctive. The public will be given a new opportunity to assess *Le Bal du comte d'Orgel* when Andrew Oliver publishes his edition of the original manuscript, comparing it with what he considers to be the heavily edited 'orthodox' published version. Grasset himself has stated, writing in 1943, that Radiguet, preoccupied with his future call-up, had told him that various words in the texts were 'provisional'. Radiguet had seemed dissatisfied with the book. His publisher found the author's attitude alarming, all the more so when at the end of their talk Radiguet insisted on giving him the scarf he was wearing, telling him to keep it *en souvenir*.

This was but one of many incidents reported by friends who have insisted that Radiguet had had premonitions of his own death, or even that he caused it by deliberate self-neglect. It is true that he seemed strangely drawn to people, women at least, with suicidal tendencies – Bolette Natanson attempted suicide more than once, and finally succeeded; Beatrice Hastings gassed herself in Worthing in 1943 – but before his illness Radiguet had seemed full of life and ideas, and had even cut down his drinking. He had started to write verse again, telling Poulenc that he hoped some of it would be suitable for setting to music. But there can be no doubt that his last year had been exhausting. It had started with the publicity campaign for his first novel; then came the strains of his new-found fame, the unexpected reappearance of Alice and Gaston, the tensions in his relationship with Cocteau. Radiguet had had five years of exhausting life, the last two of which would have taxed the strength of any writer.

He did not disappear. After his death his friends had paid his bills, Cocteau had kept many manuscripts. In 1925 there appeared a strange little book of poems, entitled *Vers libres,* published *Au panier fleuri* at Champigny, and credited to Radiguet. The poems were obscene and very funny. Their authenticity was denied at once by Radiguet's father and by Cocteau, yet strangely enough at least two of the poems *were* by Radiguet. There was a charming sexual poem called *Saison* which begins:

Bilboquet dont je suis la tige
Sur laquelle est tombé ton corps

and another, entitled *Ebauches,* which describes Venus appearing in a trouser-skirt and making love with the poet while waiting for a tram to La République. 'Making love' is a decidedly genteel translation:

En jupe-culottes
Un soir à Joinville
Vénus la salope
M'a sucé la bite

Son joli chignon
En papier doré
Me faisait bander
Comme un cuirassier

Puis nous nous branlâmes
Le con et la trique
Attendant un tram
Pour la République.

In 1925 it was understandable that those close to Radiguet would deny the authenticity of these poems, for their cheerful obscenity would hardly add to the reputation of a serious novelist. Fifty years later, and after Cocteau's death, it is just as understandable that most people have come to accept them for what they are worth. A contract has been found in France for the publication of a book of poems by Radiguet called *Jouets du vent,* of which nobody knows very much, although the phrase occurs in the poem *Avec la mort tu te maries . . .*, published in 1925. However, the writer Maurice Martin du Gard possesses a note from Radiguet giving him permission to publish his 'obscene poems', as the poet calls them. Many of his friends thought that he wrote them between 1919 and 1921 and was ready to make money out of them if he had the chance. Whoever published these poems in 1925 was obviously no friend of Cocteau, since a few lines at the beginning of the book show a jealous disapproval of the mysterious editing of Radiguet's second novel: 'We give the text of these few pieces as it appears in the papers left by Radiguet. This statement is perhaps not without value: could one be certain that *Le Bal du comte d'Orgel* was not revised and corrected by obliging people whom Radiguet had certainly not asked to carry out *la toilette des morts*?'

Radiguet will be remembered not for a small, dubious collection of erotic verse but as the very young man who put all his energy into writing – writing, as a game, especially in the theatre; writing as a critical weapon; and, most of all, writing as a means of expressing what he had seen of love in the context of different social backgrounds. The love-relationship fascinated him but brought him little happiness. He saw the cruelty that people in love – men and women, or men and men – inflicted on each other, often unconsciously, and he realized that they could not stop themselves. He was realistic, perhaps pessimistic, but just as he was anxious to go beyond the avant-garde, so he had to go beyond the starry-eyed, romantic view of love. His was a distinctive voice in the early twentieth century; now, perhaps, as Cocteau said of Picasso, time has caught up with him.

In the past, the achievements of very young people in the arts seem often to have been limited to acrobatics of the mind, such as the Latin verse which Milton composed at eighteen or before. When Aldous Huxley prefaced a translation of *Le Diable au corps* in 1932 he discussed this phenomenon and referred to the many child prodigies in the world of music, which he described as the art 'farthest from reality'. He may have read Radiguet's own words, à propos his novel, about 'having lived and starting to live', for he went on to say: 'In the realm of literature you cannot be an infant prodigy and at the same time innocent of the world. Precocious experience is a necessary condition and prerequisite of "marvellous boyhood". Chatterton's knowledge of the miseries of life was extensive. Rimbaud – by far the most highly gifted of all the marvellous boys and a poet of the first rank and of profound historical importance – Rimbaud had done and suffered more by the time he was twenty, when he abandoned literature, than most men have done and suffered in half a long life. And similarly, Raymond Radiguet, the most recent of his marvellous kind, was precociously experienced. *Le Diable au corps* is the work of a boy who has lived through many of the experiences of manhood.' Huxley found it mature, finished, complete; it had certainty, directness, swiftness and a simplicity which is 'generally the result of a long slow process of chastening and concentration and refinement. Radiguet set out in possession of those literary virtues with which most writers painfully end.'

Scientific discoveries of importance have often been made by very young men, notably by Isaac Newton, but young writers have inevitably been rarer. Although in the past many young people had 'precocious experience' – often in the army, for example – they were not usually those with the personality and education likely to turn them into poets and novelists. Some writers have made a brilliant start which they have failed to maintain, like Violet Paget, known as 'Vernon Lee', who in her early twenties wrote masterly studies of eighteenth-century Italy but is probably now best remembered for her ghost stories.

Radiguet was one of the first young writers of the twentieth century who met experience and used it immediately. His novels were and remain impressive because he possessed not only the experience but the faculty of interpreting it, bringing all his readers into it, reminding them, however different their lives and make-up, that something within them, somewhere, coincided with the thoughts and feelings of *his* characters. As time passes his case will seem less isolated than it did in the early 'twenties. Other young literary prodigies have appeared after Radiguet. Françoise Mallet-Joris, for instance, wrote *Le Rempart des Béguines,* the story of a girl in love with her father's mistress, when she was eighteen. Against a very different cultural background, Yukio Mishima wrote *Confessions of a Mask,* regarded by many as his masterpiece, at the age of twenty-three, having already written five other books. Mishima is an interesting parallel to Radiguet, not only because Radiguet was one of Mishima's heroes. He too lived through a major war, venerated the classics (of Japanese literature) rather than the avant-garde, and he too was bisexual. Mishima, like Radiguet, was hailed as a genius at a very early age, and in his case it is possible to assess the true damage caused by such early success. His critical reputation in Japan declined steadily, and it is only with *The Sea of Fertility* tetralogy, his last works before his suicide, that he found again the power and intensity of his early work.

Young people now are no longer held back from the experience that was once called 'precocious' by their over-protective or authoritarian elders. Since they write about it incessantly, their youth alone is no longer a phenomenon to be exploited by publishers' publicity departments. But a combination of youth and mature observation is still as rare as it was in Radiguet's day, and may always be so. Youth's a stuff will not endure; a 'young writer' becomes a 'writer' or he disappears, either into mediocrity, silence or death. There is no merit in dying young, and little use in speculating whether Radiguet did not want to stay alive, but his death at twenty has preserved his youth in a clear-cut if cruel way: neither he nor his work have grown old. Writers remember it and quote it; critics still discuss it; scholars analyse it; but, most important of all, the mythical 'average reader' can still enjoy it. This is why the novels of Raymond Radiguet have become classics and why François Mauriac was able to write, 'This child was a master.'

In 1945 Cocteau went back to Le Picquey with Jean Marais, the actor. He found himself living in memories as though they had been discarded the day before. He wrote to Jean Hugo and said everything was in its place. There were more houses, and mines on the beach, but 'the same pine needles, the same wooden walls, the same fishing nets, the same seaweed'. He thought he was staying in the same village where they had trimmed Radiguet's hair with an oyster shell.

During the last two years of Radiguet's life Cocteau had written poems, some of them fine, expressing his love for him, brooding nostalgically on age and death. He did not realize then how many more times death would cross his path, how many other men he would love – Marcel Khill, Jean Desbordes – were to die violently or unexpectedly. He suffered Radiguet's death, he said, like an operation without chloroform, and he wrote other deeply-felt poems about him after his death, notably *L'Ange Heurtebise,* an outstanding composition in which the concept of the 'angel poets', set out in *Le Secret professionnel,* was now identified with the man he had loved. Other, shorter poems are less important but touching in a naïve, pathetic way. Radiguet, the angel, had spent twenty years on holiday from heaven, he said, and he had not dared to tell his parents that his vocation was death. Cocteau referred to Radiguet's 'true patriotism' – for his family, the Marne and the Ile d'Amour. Students, he wrote, would ask him what he was like. Was he fair or dark? In fact his gaze was almond-like, he was like a sailor's song.

His publisher, Bernard Grasset, had met a great many writers of all ages, but he never forgot Radiguet. Looking around his office, he once described their first meeting: 'He came in that way, he sat down on that chair and for the first and only time in my life I felt certain I was in the presence of a genius.'

Raymond Radiguet survives neither as angel nor genius, but as the author of two remarkable novels, some poems and short prose pieces, and the work in progress that led up to them. This small body of work provides a glimpse, no more, of how he thought and felt . . . and of how much of life he lived in the space of a mere five years.

Select Bibliography

Two versions of Raymond Radiguet's *Oeuvres complètes* have been published, in 1952 and 1959 respectively, but neither are 'complete'. Both contain the two novels, the best of Radiguet's poems and shorter prose pieces. The Club des Libraires' two-volume edition includes various drafts and notes, some of which may also be found in David Noakes's study.

Among the MSS. owned by the author's brother, M. René Radiguet, are the first sketch for *Le Diable au corps,* five versions of the ending, and the first version of *Le Bal du comte d'Orgel.* Cocteau's heir, M. Edouard Dermith, owns the second version of *Le Bal,* MSS. of various shorter works, and letters.

The studies by Keith Goesch, David Noakes and Nadia Odouard all contain previously unpublished material: letters, articles and *Hommage à Chateaubriand* in the first, further poems in the second, in addition to various drafts and notes found after Radiguet's death in the dossier labelled *Désordres.* Nadia Odouard, in *Les Années folles de Raymond Radiguet,* quotes from the manuscript sources listed above. Appendices to her book include the following MSS.: some material from the first version of *Le Diable au corps,* and a list of editorial corrections to it by Abel Hermant; passages subsequently omitted from *Le Bal du comte d'Orgel*; eleven short poems; the letters to Radiguet from Beatrice Hastings, which had remained in Cocteau's possession, together with a letter from her to Cocteau, and a poem by her; and, finally, letters from various other correspondents addressed to Radiguet and one from Georges Vidal to Cocteau.

The *Cahiers Jean Cocteau 2* published for the first time the complete libretto of *Le Gendarme incompris.* No. 4 of the *Cahiers* includes some unpublished letters from Radiguet to Madame Cocteau, and *Une Soirée mémorable,* written jointly by Radiguet and Cocteau.

For a more detailed bibliography than the one which follows, the reader is referred to Nadia Odouard's study.

I WORKS BY RAYMOND RADIGUET

Oeuvres complètes, Grasset, Paris, 1952.
Oeuvres complètes, 2 vols., Club des Libraires, Paris, 1959.
Règle du Jeu, preface by Jean Cocteau, Editions du Rocher, Monaco, 1957.
Gli inediti, ed. Liliana Garuti delli Ponti, preface by Luigi de Nardis, Parma, 1967. (Includes *La Ville au lac d'argent,* parts of *Paul et Virginie,* and some of the poems from *Jeux innocents.*)
Le Bal du comte d'Orgel, integral text of the first MS, entitled by Radiguet *Le Fantôme du devoir,* edited by Andrew Oliver, forthcoming; Mr Oliver has also edited a critical edition of *Le Bal,* using Radiguet's uncut, final text: forthcoming.

IN ENGLISH

The Devil in the Flesh, trans. Kay Boyle, preface by Aldous Huxley, Black Sun Press, Paris, 1932; Harrison Smith, New York, 1932; Grey Walls Press, London, 1949.
The Devil in the Flesh, trans. Alan Sheridan Smith, Calder & Boyars, London, 1971.
Devil in the Flesh, trans. and with an introduction by Robert Baldick, Penguin, Harmondsworth, 1971.
Ball at Count d'Orgel's, trans. Malcolm Cowley, Norton, New York, 1929.
Count d'Orgel Opens the Ball, trans. Violet Schiff, Harvill Press, London, 1952.
Count d'Orgel, trans. Alan Sheridan Smith, Calder & Boyars, London, 1969.
Cheeks on Fire, Collected Poems, trans. Alan Stone, John Calder, London, 1976.
The Pelicans, in Michael Benedikt and George E. Wellworth (eds.), *Modern French Plays,* Faber & Faber, 1965.
The Flower-Girl, Harper's Bazaar, No. 2862, New York, 1950.

II WORKS ABOUT RAYMOND RADIGUET

BOOKS

Borgal, Clément, *Radiguet,* Editions Universitaires, Paris, 1969.
Cocteau, Jean, *Le Rappel à l'ordre,* Stock, Paris, 1926; trans. Rollo Myers ('Order Considered as Anarchy') in Margaret Crosland (ed.), *Cocteau's World,* Peter Owen, London, 1972.

Cocteau, Jean, *La Difficulté d'être,* Editions du Rocher, Monaco, 1953; trans. Elizabeth Sprigge (*The Difficulty of Being*), Peter Owen, London, 1967.

Goesch, Keith, *Raymond Radiguet,* Editions de la Palatine, Paris/Geneva, 1955.

Noakes, David, *Raymond Radiguet,* Pierre Seghers, Paris, 1969.

Odouard, Nadia, *Les années folles de Raymond Radiguet,* Pierre Seghers, Paris, 1974.

ARTICLES ETC.

A Saint-Maur, dans les Années 20 . . . Raymond Radiguet, Bulletin hors série, Saint-Maur, February, 1974.

Cahiers Jean Cocteau, Nos. 1-5, Gallimard, Paris, 1969-1975.

Leighton, Lawrence, 'An Autopsy and a Prescription', *Hound and Horn,* Concord, New Hampshire, July-September 1932.

Oliver, Andrew, '*Le bal du comte d'Orgel: structure, mythe, signification*', *Revue des Langues Romanes,* LXXXI, 1975.

Rivière, Jacques, '*Le Bal du comte d'Orgel*', *N.R.F.,* Paris, July 1924.

Turnell, Martin, 'Raymond Radiguet *ou les bizarreries du coeur*', *Cornhill Magazine,* No. 970, Spring 1947.

Wyndham, Francis, 'Raymond Radiguet', *Sunday Times Magazine,* 29 January, 1967.

III OTHER WORKS CONSULTED

Fay, Bernard, *Les Précieux,* Librairie académique Perrin, Paris, 1966.

Germain, André, *De Proust à Dada,* Kra, Paris, 1924.

Hamnett, Nina, *Laughing Torso,* Constable, London, 1932.

Kihm, Jean-Jacques, Sprigge, Elizabeth, and Béhar, Henri C., *Jean Cocteau,* La Table Ronde,Paris, 1968.

Magny, Claude-Edmonde, *Histoire du roman français depuis 1918,* Editions du Seuil, Paris, 1950.

Milhaud, Darius, *Notes Without Music,* Dennis Dobson, London, 1952.

Poulenc, Francis, *Correspondence 1915-1963,* Editions du Seuil, Paris, 1967.

Raymond, Marcel, *From Baudelaire to Surrealism,* Peter Owen, London, 1957.

'Sem', *La Ronde de Nuit,* Fayard, Paris, 1923.

Sichel, Pierre, *Modigliani,* W. H. Allen, London, 1967.

Steegmuller, Francis, *Cocteau,* Macmillan, London, 1969.

Turnell, Martin, *The Novel in France,* Hamish Hamilton, London, 1958.

Index

References to Radiguet's individual works have been listed under his name.